CONTENTS

For pattern inquiries, please visit: www.go-crafty.com

LITTLE CUTIES BLANKETS

YARN

Bernat® *Baby Coordinates™ Solids* 5oz/140g skeins, each approx 388yd/355m; *White* 5oz/140g skeins, each approx 475yd/418m (acrylic/rayon/nylon)

BOY'S VERSION

- MC #48128 Soft Blue 4 skeins
- CC #48005 White 2 skeins

GIRL'S VERSION

- MC #48420 Baby Pink 4 skeins
- CC #48005 White 2 skeins

HOOK

- Size G-6 (4mm) crochet hook *or size needed to obtain gauge*

MEASUREMENTS

Boy's Version: Approximately 37 x 45" [94 x 114cm]

Girl's Version: Approximately 39 x 47" [99 x 119.5cm]

GAUGE

One Motif A or B = 4½" [11.5cm] square. *Take time to check gauge.*

MOTIF A (MAKE 40)

With MC, ch 4. Join with sl st to first ch to form a ring.

1st rnd: Ch 4 (counts as dc and ch 1). (1 dc. Ch 1) 11 times into ring. Join with sl st to 3rd ch of ch 4. 12 dc. Fasten off.

2nd rnd: Join A with sl st into any ch 1 sp. Ch 3. (Yoh and draw up a loop in same sp as last sl st. Yoh and draw through 2 loops on hook) twice. Yoh and draw through all loops on hook—counts as Cluster. [Ch 3. (Yoh and draw up a loop. Yoh and draw through 2 loops on hook) 3 times in next ch 1 sp. Yoh and draw yarn through all loops on hook—Cluster made] 11 times. Ch 3. Join with sl st to top of first Cluster. Fasten off.

3rd rnd: Join MC with sl st to any ch 3 sp. Ch 1. 1 sc in same sp. (Ch 5. 1 sc in next ch 3 sp) 11 times. Ch 2. 1 dc in first sc. Fasten off.

4th rnd: Join A with sl st to sp where last dc was made. Ch 1. 1 sc in last dc. *Ch 5. 1 sc in next ch 5 sp. Ch 1. (5 dc. Ch 3. 5 dc) all in next ch 5 sp. Ch 1. 1 sc in next ch 5 sp. Rep from * 3 times more omitting 1 sc at end of last rep. Join with sl st to first sc. Fasten off.

MOTIF B (MAKE 40)

With MC, ch 22.

Foundation row: (RS) 1 sc in 2nd ch from hook. *Ch 1. Sk next ch. 1 sc in next ch. Rep from * to end of ch. Ch 1. Turn.

1st row: 1 sc in first sc. *1 sc in next ch 1 sp. Ch 1. Sk next sc. Rep from * to last 2 sts. 1 sc in next ch 1 sp. 1 sc in last sc. Ch 1. Turn.

2nd row: 1 sc in first sc. *Ch 1. Sk next sc. 1 sc in next ch 1 sp. Rep from * to last 2 sts. Ch 1. Sk next sc. 1 sc in last sc. Ch 1. Turn.

Rep last 2 rows 8 times more, omitting turning ch at end of last row. (19 rows total). Fasten off.

FINISHING

Join motifs into 8 strips 10 motifs long alternating Motif A and Motif B as illustrated, as follows: With RS facing each other, join MC with sl st through corresponding corner. Working through both thicknesses, ch 1. 1 sc in same sp. *1 sc in next st. Ch 1. Sk next st. Rep from * across. 1 sc through next corresponding corner.

Join Strips in the same manner as Motifs.

GIRL'S VERSION ONLY

EDGING

1st rnd: Join A with sl st to any corner of Blanket. Ch 1. 1 sc in same sp as sl st. *Work 16 sc along side of next Motif. 1 sc between Motifs. Rep from * around, working 3 sc in corners of Blanket and ending with 2 sc in last corner. Join with sl st to first sc. Fasten off.

2nd rnd: Join MC with sl st to any corner sc. Ch 1. (1 sc. Ch 3. 1 sc) all in same sp as last sl st. [*Ch 3. Sk next sc. 1 sc in next sc. Rep from * to next corner sc. (1 sc. Ch 3. 1 sc) all in next corner sc] twice. **Ch 3. Sk

next sc. 1 sc in next sc. Rep from ** to next corner sc. Ch 3. Join with sl st to first sc.

3rd rnd: Sl st to next ch 3 sp. Ch 1. 1 sc in same sp. *Ch 3. 1 sc in next ch 3 sp. Rep from * around. Ch 3. Join with sl st to first sc. Fasten off.

4th rnd: Join A with sl st to any ch 3 sp. Ch 1. 1 sc in same sp. *Ch 5. Sl st in 3rd ch of ch 5 – Picot made. Ch 1. 1 sc in next ch 3 sp. Rep from * around. Picot. Ch 1. Join with sl st to first sc. Fasten off.

BOY'S VERSION ONLY

EDGING

With A, work 1st rnd as given for Girl's Version.

2nd rnd: Join MC with sl st to any corner sc. Ch 1. Working from left to right instead of from right to left, as usual, work 1 sc in each sc around for reverse sc. Join with sl st to first sc. Fasten off. ■

reverse sc

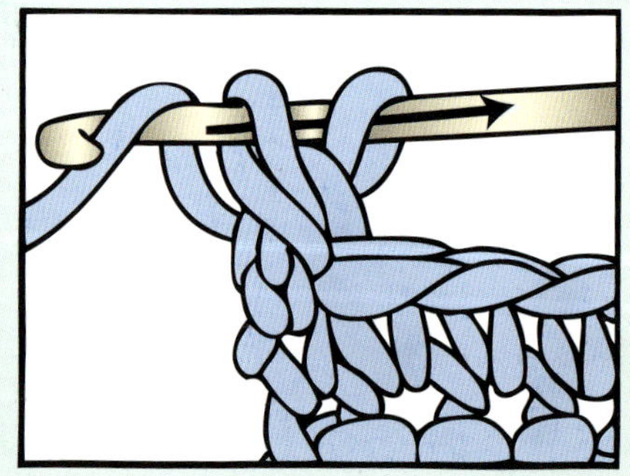

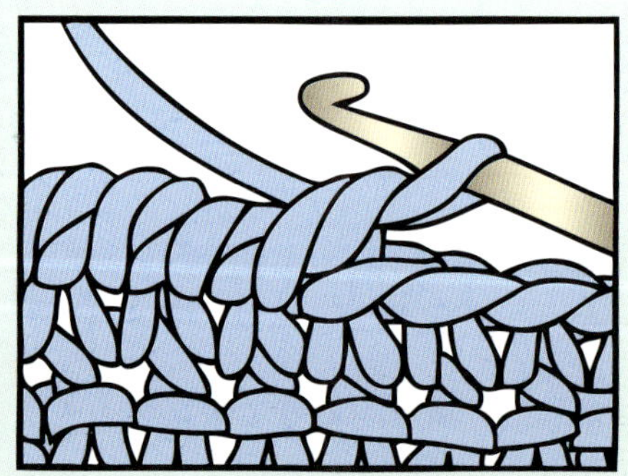

SWEETHEARTS BLANKETS

YARN 2

Bernat® *Baby Coordinates*™ *Solids* 5oz/140g skeins, each approx 388yd/355m; *White* 5oz/140g skeins, each approx 475yd/418m (acrylic/rayon/nylon)

BOY'S VERSION

- MC #48005 White 3 skeins
- A #48738 Soft Turquoise 2 skeins
- B #48128 Soft Blue 2 skeins
- C #48615 Lemon Custard 2 skeins
- D #48228 Iced Mint 2 skeins

GIRL'S VERSION

- MC #48005 White 3 skeins
- A #48420 Baby Pink 2 skeins
- B #48512 Sherbert 2 skeins
- C #48615 Lemon Custard 2 skeins
- D #48320 Soft Mauve 2 skeins

HOOK

- Size G-6 (4mm) crochet hook *or size needed to obtain gauge*

MEASUREMENTS

Approximately 36 x 48" [91.5 x 122cm].

GAUGE

One Motif = 12" [30.5cm] square. *Take time to check gauge.*

MOTIF (MAKE 12)

With MC, ch 38.

1st row: (RS) 1 dc in 6th ch from hook (counts as dc and ch 1). *Ch 1. Sk next ch. 1 dc in next ch. Rep from * to end of row. Turn.

Beg with WS, work Chart I to end of Chart reading RS rows from right to left and WS rows from left to right. Ch 8 at end of last row for extended ch 8. Fasten off.

Note: See Edging Diagram for placement.

EDGING A

With RS of work facing, join A with sl st to top right corner.

1st row: Ch 3 (counts as dc). Sk first dc. Work 34 dc evenly across top of Motif. Work 1 dc in each of next 8 ch. 43 dc. Turn.

2nd row: Ch 3 (counts as dc). Work 1 dc in each dc to end of row. Turn. Rep last row twice more. Fasten off.

EDGING B

With RS of work facing, join B with sl st to bottom right corner of Motif.

1st row: Ch 3 (counts as dc). Work a further 42 dc evenly up right side of work. Turn.

2nd row: Ch 3 (counts as dc). Work 1 dc in each dc to end of row. Turn. Rep last row twice more. Fasten off.

EDGING C

With RS of work facing, join C with sl st to bottom left corner of work.

1st row: Ch 3 (counts as dc). Work a further 42 dc evenly across bottom of work. Turn.

2nd row: Ch 3 (counts as dc). Work 1 dc in each dc to end of row. Turn.

Rep last row twice more. Fasten off.

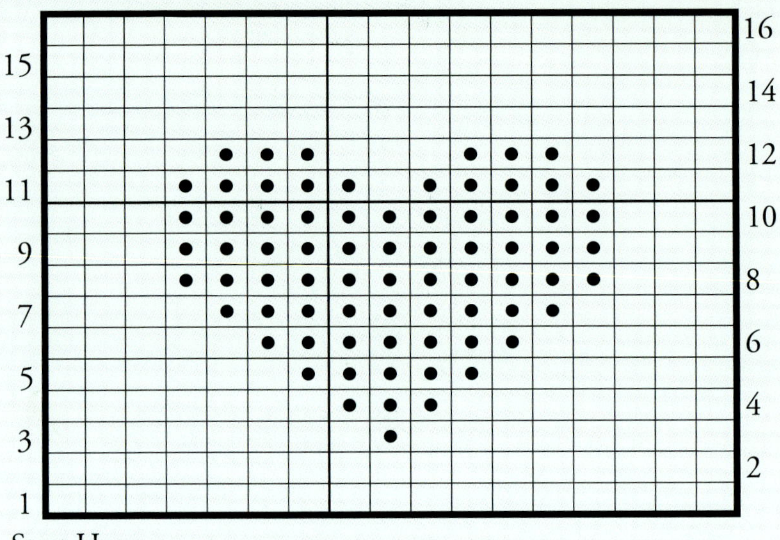

Key

Note: Ch 3 at beg of row not shown on chart.

☐ = Ch 1. Sk next st. 1 dc in next st.

⊡ = 1 dc in each of next 2 sts.

EDGING D

With RS of work facing, join D with sl st to top left corner of Motif (leave extended ch 8 unworked).

1st row: Ch 3 (counts as dc). Work a further 42 dc evenly down left side of work. Turn.

2nd row: Ch 3 (counts as dc). Work 1 dc in each dc to end of row. Turn.

Rep last row twice more. Fasten off.

Sew opening closed (created by ch 8 extension and Edging D (see diagram).

FINISHING

Join Motifs into 3 strips, 4 Motifs long as follows: With RS facing each other, join appropriate color with sl st through corresponding corner. Working through both thicknesses, ch 1. 1 sc in same sp. *1 sc in next st. Ch 1. Sk next st. Rep from * across. 1 sc through corresponding corner.

Join Strips in the same manner as Motifs. ■

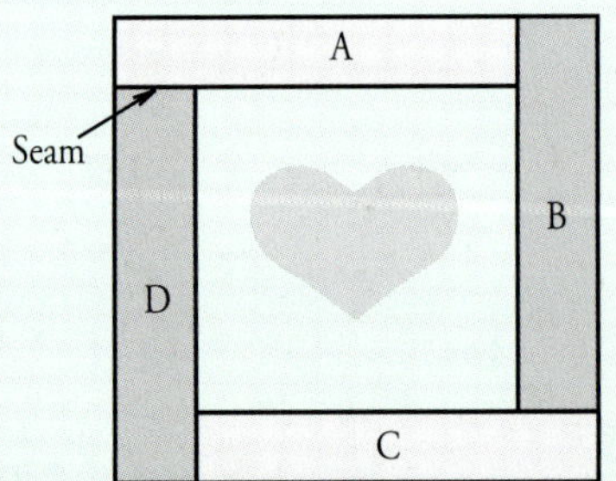

FUZZY FLOWERS BLANKET

YARN (5)

Bernat® *Pipsqueak*™
3½oz/100g skeins, each approx 120yd/109m (polyester)

- MC #59005 Whitey White 3 skeins
- A #59420 Pretty Pink 3 skeins
- B #59415 Candy Girl 3 skeins

HOOK

Size K-10½ (6.5m) crochet hook *or size needed to obtain gauge*

MEASUREMENTS

Approx 38" [96.5cm] square

GAUGE

Motif = Approx 5½" [14cm] corner to corner. *Take time to check gauge.*

BLANKET

MOTIF A (MAKE 36)

Note Follow chart or written instructions below.

With A, ch 4. Join with sl st to form a ring.

1st rnd: Ch 1. 6 sc in ring. Join with sl st to first sc.

2nd rnd: Ch 3. (Yoh and draw up a loop. Yoh and draw through 2 loops on hook) twice in same sp as last sl st. Yoh and draw through all loops on hook – counts as cluster. *Ch 3. (Yoh and draw up a loop. Yoh and draw through 2 loops on hook) 3 times in next sc. Yoh and draw through all loops on hook – cluster made. Rep from * 4 times more. Ch 3. Join with sl st to top of first cluster. Break A.

3rd rnd: Join MC with sl st in any ch-3 sp. Ch 4 (counts as dc and ch 1). (1 dc. Ch 3. 1 dc. Ch 1. 1 dc) in same sp as sl st. *Ch 1. (1 dc. Ch 1. 1 dc. Ch 3. 1 dc. Ch 1. 1 dc) in next ch-3 sp. Rep from * 4 times more. Ch 1. Join with sl st to 3rd ch of ch 4. Fasten off.

MOTIF B (MAKE 9)

Work as for Motif A, substituting B for A and A for MC.

FINISHING

Join Motifs tog into 7 strips as shown in diagram as follows:

Joining 2 Motifs: With RS of Motifs facing tog, join MC on WS through corresponding corner ch-3 sps. Ch 1. 1 sc in same sp. *Ch 2. 1 sc through next corresponding ch-1 sps. Rep from *, ending with ch 2. 1 sc through next corresponding corner ch-3 sps. Fasten off.

Join Strips of Motifs tog in same manner.

EDGING

Join A with sl st in any corner ch-3 sp. Ch 1. 3 sc in same sp. Work sc evenly around outer edge of Blanket, working 3 sc in each ch-3 corner sp. Join with sl st to first sc. Fasten off. ■

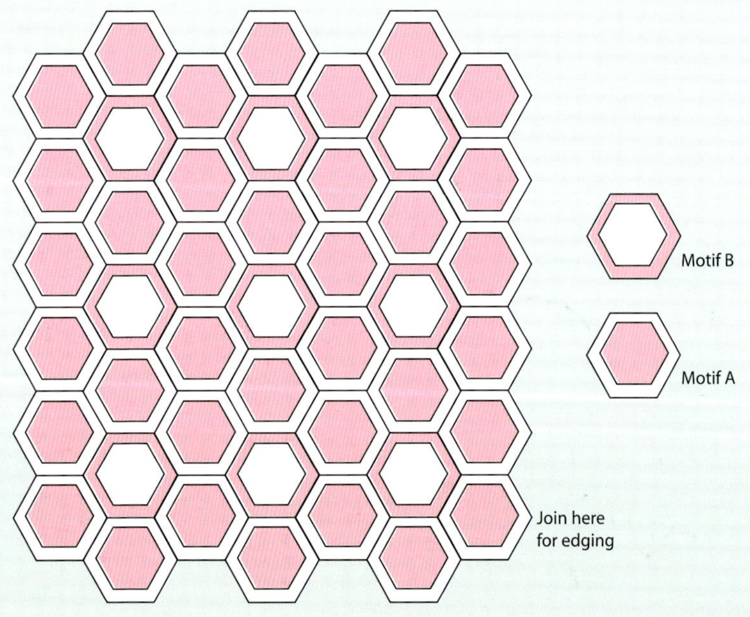

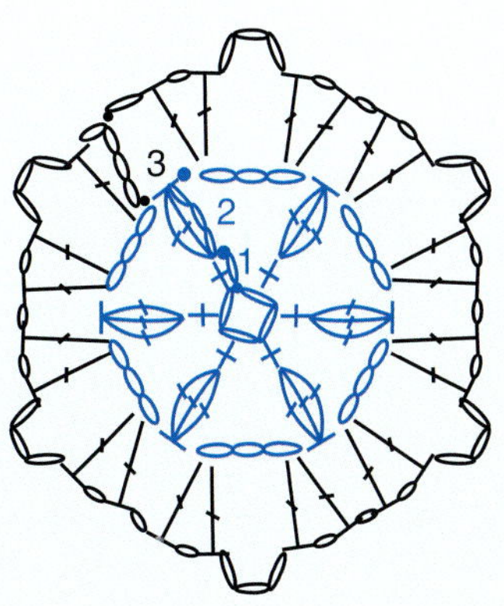

• = slip stitch (sl st)
⬭ = chain (ch)
┼ = single crochet (sc)
⫪ = double crochet (dc)
⦶ = cluster

HARLEQUIN BLANKET

YARN (3)

Bernat® *Softee® Baby™ Solids* 5oz/140g skeins, each approx 362yd/331m;
Ombres 4oz/120g skeins, each approx 392yd/358m (acrylic)

- MC #30184 Baby Denims 2 skeins
- A #30185 Soft Lilac 2 skeins
- B #31302 Her Jeans Ombre 1 skein

HOOK

- Size 7 (4.5mm) crochet hook *or size needed to obtain gauge*

MEASUREMENTS

Approx 31 x 39" [80 x 99cm]

GAUGE

One Motif = 6" [16.5cm] square.
Take time to check gauge.

MOTIF 1 (MAKE 20)

With A, ch 2.

1st rnd: 6 sc in 2nd ch from hook. Join with sl st to first sc.

2nd rnd: Ch 1. 2 sc in each sc around. Join MC with sl st to first sc. 12 sc.

3rd rnd: With MC, ch 1, working into back loop only of each st around. *2 sc in next sc. 1 sc in next sc. Rep from * around. Join with sl st to first sc. 18 sc.

4th rnd: Ch 3. 1 dc in same sc as last sl st. *1 dc in next sc. 2 dc in next sc. Rep from * to last sc. 2 dc in last sc. Join with sl st to top of ch 3. 28 dc.

5th rnd: Ch 3. 4 dc in same sp as last sl st. *1 dc in each of next 6 dc. 5 dc in next dc. Rep from * twice more. 1 dc in each of last 6 dc. Join with sl st to top of ch 3.

6th rnd: Ch 3. Sk first dc. 1 dc in next dc. *5 dc in next dc. 1 dc in each of next 10 dc. Rep from * twice more. 5 dc in next dc. 1 dc in each of last 8 dc. Join A with sl st to top of ch 3.

7th rnd: With A, ch 1. 1 sc in same sp as last sl st. 1 sc in each of next 3 dc. *3 sc in next dc. 1 sc in each of next 7 dc. 2 sc in next dc. 1 sc in each of next 6 dc. Rep fom * twice more. 3 sc in next dc. 1 sc in each of next 6 dc. 2 sc in next dc. 1 sc in each of last 3 dc. Join B with sl st to first sc.

8th rnd: With B, sl st in next sc. Ch 2. (Yoh and draw up a loop) 3 times in next sc. Yoh and draw through 6 loops on hook. Yoh and draw through rem 2 loops on hook – bobble made. Ch 1. Sk next sc. Bobble in next sc. Ch 1. Sk next sc. *(Bobble. Ch 1. Bobble) all in next corner sc. (Ch 1. Sk next sc. Bobble in next sc) 8 times. Rep from * twice more. Ch 1. Sk next sc. (Bobble. Ch

1. Bobble) in next corner sc. (Ch 1. Sk next sc. Bobble in next sc) 6 times. Ch 1. Join A with sl st to top of ch 2.

9th rnd: With A, ch 1. 1 sc in each st or ch 1 sp around, working 3 sc in corner ch 1 sps. Join with sl st to first sc. Fasten off.

MOTIF 2 (MAKE 12)

Work as given for Motif 1, substituting MC for A in rnds 1, 2, 7 and 9; and substituting A for MC in rnds 3 to 6.

Following diagram, crochet Motifs tog with MC.

Outer Edging: With RS of work facing, join MC with sl st to side edge of Blanket at top corner. Work 1 row of sc evenly around outer edge of Blanket. Join with sl st to first sc.

Next rnd: Working from left to right instead of from right to left, as usual, work 1 reverse sc in each sc around. Join with sl st to first sc. Fasten off. ■

RIPPLE BLANKET

YARN

Bernat® *Baby Coordinates™ Solids* 5oz/140g skeins, each approx 388yd/355m; *White* 5oz/140g skeins, each approx 475yd/418m (acrylic/rayon/nylon)

- A #48005 White 2 skeins
- B #48128 Soft Blue 1 skein
- C #48420 Baby Pink 1 skein
- D #48615 Lemon Custard 1 skein
- E #48228 Iced Mint 1 skein

HOOK

- Size H-8 (5mm) crochet hook *or size needed to obtain gauge*

MEASUREMENTS

Approximately 36 x 40" [91.5 x 101.5cm]

GAUGE

14 sc and 15 rows = 4" [10cm]. *Take time to check gauge.*

BLANKET

With B, ch 139.

1st row: (RS) 2 dc in 4th ch from hook (counts as 3 dc). (2 dc in next ch) twice. (Sk next ch. 1 dc in next ch) 5 times. *Sk next ch. (2 dc in next ch) 6 times. (Sk next ch. 1 dc in next ch) 5 times. Rep from * to last 4 ch. Sk next ch. (2 dc in next ch) 3 times. Turn.

2nd row: Ch 1. 1 sc in each dc across. 1 sc in top of turning ch. Join A. Turn. 137 sc.

3rd row: With A, ch 3 (counts as dc). (2 dc in next sc) 3 times. (Sk next sc. 1 dc in next sc) 5 times. *Sk next sc. (2 dc in next sc) 6 times. (Sk next sc. 1 dc in next sc) 5 times. Rep from * to last 4 sc. Sk next sc. (2 dc in next sc) 3 times. Turn.

4th row: Ch 1. 1 sc in each dc across. 1 sc in top of turning ch. Join B. Turn.

Rep 3rd and 4th rows for Zig-Zag Pat in Stripes as follows:

2 rows B. 2 rows A. 2 rows C. 2 rows A. 2 rows D. 2 rows A. 2 rows D. 2 rows A. 2 rows C. 2 rows A. 2 rows E. 2 rows A. 2 rows E. 2 rows A. 2 rows D. 2 rows A. 2 rows B. 2 rows A.

Rep from ** to ** (36 rows) for Stripe Pat once more. Work 2 rows B. Fasten off. ■

PUFFY BLANKET

YARN

Bernat® *Baby Blanket*™
3½oz/100g skeins, each approx 86yd/78m (polyester)
• #03615 Baby Yellow 7 skeins

HOOK

• Size P/15 (12mm) crochet hook *or size needed to obtain gauge*

MEASUREMENTS

Approximately 35" [89cm] square

GAUGE

3 Clusters and 3 rows = 4" [10cm] in pat. *Take time to check gauge.*

STITCH GLOSSARY

Cluster (Yoh and draw up a loop) 3 times in same stitch or space. Yoh and draw through all loops on hook.

BLANKET

Ch 52.

1st row: Cluster in 4th ch from hook. *Ch 1. Sk next ch. Cluster in next ch. Rep from * to last 2 ch. Ch 1. Sk next ch. 1 dc in last ch. Turn.

2nd row: Ch 3 (counts as dc). Sk first dc. Cluster in next ch-1 sp. *Ch 1. Sk next cluster. Cluster in next ch-1 sp. Rep from * to end of row, ending with ch 1. Sk last cluster. 1 dc in top of turning ch. Turn.

Rep 2nd row for pat until Blanket measures 35" [89 cm]. Do not fasten off.

Edging: Ch 1. Working around outside edge of Blanket, work 1 rnd of sc, having 3 sc in each corner. Join with sl st to first sc. Fasten off. ■

FROM THE MIDDLE BLANKET

YARN
Bernat® *Baby Blanket*™
3½oz/100g skeins, each
approx 86yd/78m (polyester)
• A #03202 Baby Blue 2 skeins
• B #03005 White 3 skeins
• C #03615 Baby Yellow
2 skeins

HOOK
• Size N/15 (10mm) crochet
hook *or size needed to obtain gauge*

MEASUREMENTS

Approximately 36" [91.5cm] square

GAUGE

6 dc and 4 rows = 4" [10cm].
Take time to check gauge.

BLANKET

Note: Ch 3 - count as dc.

With A, ch 4. Join with sl st to form ring.

1st rnd: Ch 1. (1 sc. Ch 3) 4 times in ring. Join with sl st to first sc.

2nd rnd: Sl st in next ch-3 sp. Ch 3. (2 dc. Ch 3. 3 dc) in same sp as last sl st. *(3 dc. Ch 3. 3 dc) in next ch-3 sp. Rep from * twice more. Join with sl st to top of ch 3. Fasten off.

3rd rnd: Join B with sl st to any corner ch-3 sp. Ch 1. (1 sc. Ch 3. 1 sc) in same sp. *Ch 3. Sk next 2 dc. 1 sc between next 2 dc. Ch 3.** (1 sc. Ch 3. 1 sc) in next corner ch-3 sp. Rep from * twice more, then from * to ** once more. Join with sl st to first sc.

4th rnd: Sl st to next ch-3 sp. Ch 3. (2 dc. Ch 3. 3 dc) in same sp. *(3 dc in next ch-3 sp) twice.** (3 dc. Ch 3. 3 dc) in next corner ch-3 sp. Rep from * twice more, then from * to ** once more. Join with sl st to top of ch 3. Fasten off.

5th rnd: Join C with sl st to any corner ch-3 sp. Ch 1. (1 sc. Ch 3. 1 sc) in same sp. *(Ch 3. Sk next 2 dc. 1 sc between next 2 dc) 3 times.** Ch 3. (1 sc. Ch 3. 1 sc) in next corner ch-3 sp. Rep from * twice more, then from * to ** once more. Ch 3. Join with sl st to first sc.

6th rnd: Sl st in next corner ch-3 sp. Ch 3. (2 dc. Ch 3. 3 dc) in same sp. *3 dc in each ch-3 sp to next corner ch-3 sp. (3 dc. Ch 3. 3 dc) in next corner ch-3 sp. Rep from * around, ending with 3 dc in last ch-3 sp. Join with sl st to top of ch 3. Fasten off.

7th rnd: Join B with sl st to any corner ch-3 sp. Ch 1. (1 sc. Ch 3. 1 sc) in same sp. *(Ch 3. Sk next 2 dc. 1 sc between next 2 dc) 5 times.** Ch 3. (1 sc. Ch 3. 1 sc) in next corner ch-3 sp. Rep from * twice more, then from * to ** once more. Ch 3. Join with sl st to first sc.

8th rnd: Sl st in next corner ch-3 sp. Ch 3. (2 dc. Ch 3. 3 dc) in same sp. *3 dc in each ch-3 sp to next corner ch-3 sp. (3 dc. Ch 3. 3 dc) in next corner ch-3 sp. Rep from * around, ending with 3 dc in last ch-3 sp. Join with sl st to top of ch 3. Fasten off.

Cont as established, working 2 rnds each in the following color sequence: A, B, C, B until Blanket from middle measures approx 18" [45.5 cm], ending with 2 rnds of any color. Fasten off. ■

WHEELS 'N WINGS BLANKETS

YARN (2)

Bernat® *Baby Coordinates*™ *Solids* 5oz/140g skeins, each approx 388yd/355m; *White* 5oz/140g skeins, each approx 475yd/418m (acrylic/rayon/nylon)

BOY'S CAR VERSION

- MC #48005 White 4 skeins
- A #48128 Blue 2 skeins
- B #48615 Lemon Custard 2 skeins

GIRL'S BUTTERFLY VERSION

- MC #48005 White 4 skeins
- A #48320 Soft Mauve 2 skeins
- B #48615 Lemon Custard 2 skeins

HOOKS

- Sizes F/5 (3.75mm) and G/6 (4mm) crochet hooks *or size needed to obtain gauge*

MEASUREMENTS

Approximately 36 x 43" [91.5 x 109cm]

GAUGE

15 dc and 7 rows = 4" [10cm] with larger hook. *Take time to check gauge.*

NOTE

To change colors, draw new color through last 2 loops of previous color as indicated.

BLANKET

STRIPED MOTIF (MAKE 10)

With MC, ch 32.

1st row: (RS) 1 dc in 4th ch from hook. 1 dc in each ch to end of ch. Ch 3. Turn. 30 sts.

2nd row: Sk first dc. 1 dc in each dc to end of row, ending with 1 dc in 3rd ch of turning ch. Join B. Ch 1. Turn.

3rd row: With B, 1 sc in each dc to end of row, ending with 1 sc in top of turning ch. Ch 1. Turn.

4th row: 1 sc in each sc to end of row. Join MC. Ch 3. Turn.

5th row: With MC, sk first sc. 1 dc in each sc to end of row. Ch 3. Turn.

Rep 2nd to 5th rows 4 times more, then 2nd row once (22 rows in all). Fasten off.

CHECKED MOTIF (MAKE 10)

With MC, ch 32.

1st row: (RS) 1 dc in 4th ch from hook. 1 dc in next ch joining A. *With A, 1 dc in each of next 3 ch, joining MC in last dc. With MC, 1 dc in each of next 3 ch, joining A in last dc. Rep from * to last 3 ch. With A, 1 dc in each of last 3 ch. Join MC. Ch 3. Turn. 30 sts.

2nd row: With MC, sk first dc. 1 dc in each of next 2 dc, joining A in last dc. *With A, 1 dc in each of next 3 dc, joining MC in last dc. With MC, 1 dc in each of next 3 dc, joining A in last dc. Rep from * to last 3 dc. With A, 1 dc in each of next 2 dc. 1 dc in top of turning ch. Join MC. Ch 3. Turn.

3rd row: With MC, sk first dc. 1 dc in each of next 2 dc, joining A in last dc. *With A, 1 dc in each of next 3 dc, joining MC in last dc. With MC, 1 dc in each of next 3 dc, joining A in last dc. Rep from * to last 3 dc. With A, 1 dc in each of next 2 dc. 1 dc in top of turning ch. Join MC. Ch 3. Turn.

Rep last 2 rows 6 times more (15 rows in all). Fasten off.

BOY'S CAR VERSION

CAR (MAKE 10)

With smaller hook and A, ch 20.

1st rnd: 4 dc in 4th ch from hook. 1 dc in each of next 15 ch. 5 dc in last ch. Working into rem loop on opposite side of ch, work 1 dc in each of next 15 ch. Join with sl st to top of ch 3.

2nd rnd: Ch 1. 1 sc in same sp as last sl st. 1 sc in next dc. 3 sc in next dc. 1 sc in each of next 19 dc. 3 sc in next dc. 1 sc in each of next 5 dc. Ch 5. Sk next 2 dc. (Yoh) 3 times. Yoh and draw up a loop in next dc. (Yoh and draw through 2 loops on hook) 4 times—long tr made. Long tr in next dc. Ch 3. Sk next 4 dc. Long tr in next dc. Work 5 sc down side of long tr just made. 1 sc in each of next 3 dc. Join with sl st to first sc. Fasten off.

With RS of work facing, join A to last sc worked before ch 5 of 2nd rnd.

WHEELS 'N WINGS BLANKETS

Work 1 sc in each of next 5 ch. 1 sc in each of next 2 long tr. 1 sc in each of next 3 ch. Join with sl st to next sc. Fasten off.

TIRES (MAKE 20)

With smaller hook and B, ch 2.

1st rnd: 6 sc in 2nd ch from hook. Join with sl st to first sc.

2nd rnd: Ch 1. 2 sc in all sl st around. Join with sl st to first sc.

3rd rnd: Ch 1. 2 sc in first sc. *1 sc in next sc. 2 sc in next sc. Rep from * to last sc. 1 sc in last sc. Join with sl st to first sc. Fasten off.

Sew Cars and Tires in position to Striped Motifs as illustrated.

Following Diagram, sew Motifs into Strips, then sew Strips into Blanket.

EDGING

1st rnd: With RS of work facing, join B with sl st to any corner. Work 1 rnd sc evenly around Afghan, working 3 sc in corners. Join A with sl st to first sc.

2nd rnd: With A, ch 3. 1 dc in each sc around, working 5 dc in corners. Join with sl st to top of ch 3.

3rd rnd: Working from left to right instead of from right to left as usual, work 1 reverse sc in each sc around. Join with sl st to first sc. Fasten off.

GIRL'S BUTTERFLY VERSION

BUTTERFLY (MAKE 10)

With A and smaller hook, ch 10. Join in rnd with sl st in first ch.

1st rnd: Ch 1. [(1 sc. Ch 9. 2 sc) all in ring] twice. [(1 sc. Ch 5. 2 sc) all in ring] twice. Join with sl st in first sc.

2nd rnd: *Sl st in next ch 9 sp. (Ch 3. 4 dc. 5 tr. 5 dc) all in same ch 9 sp. Sl st in each of next 3 sc. Rep from

* once more. (9 dc in next ch 5 sp. Sl st in each of next 3 sc) twice. Fasten off.

3rd rnd: Join B with sl st in last sl st. *1 sc in top of next ch 3. 1 sc in each of next 5 sts. 3 sc in each of next 3 sts. 1 sc in each of next 6 sts. Sl st in each of next 3 sts. Rep from * once more. **1 sc in each of next 2 sts. 3 sc in each of next 2 sts. (1 sc. Ch 3. Sl st in first ch – picot made. 1 sc) all in next st. 3 sc in each of next 2 sts. 1 sc in each of next 2 sts. ** Sl st in each of next 3 sts. Rep from ** to **. Sl st in each of next 2 sts. Join with sl st to first st. Fasten off.

BODY AND ANTENNAE (MAKE 10)

With B and smaller hook, ch 20. 3 sc in 3rd ch from hook. Sl st in each of next 9 ch. Ch 13. 3 sc in 3rd ch from hook. Sl st in each of next 9 ch. 1 sc in each of next 7 ch. 3 sc in last ch. Working into rem side of foundation ch, work 1 sc in each of next 7 ch. Fasten off.

With WS of Butterfly facing, sew foundation ch along center vertically closed. With RS of Butterfly facing, sew Body to center of Butterfly. Sew a Butterfly to center of each Checked Motif as illustrated. ■

Checked	Striped	Checked	Striped
Striped	Checked	Striped	Checked
Checked	Striped	Checked	Striped
Striped	Checked	Striped	Checked
Checked	Striped	Checked	Striped

LACE-BORDER BLANKET

YARN

Bernat® *Baby Coordinates*™ *Solids* 5oz/140g skeins, each approx 388yd/355m (acrylic/rayon/nylon)

• #01002 Lemon 3 skeins

HOOK

• Size G-6 (4mm) crochet hook *or size needed to obtain gauge*

MEASUREMENTS

Approximately 32" [81.5cm] wide x 32" [81.5 cm] long

GAUGE

5 V-sts and 8 rows = 4" [10cm] in pat. *Take time to check gauge.*

BLANKET

Ch 112.

1st row: (RS) (1 dc. Ch 2. 1 dc) in next ch - V-st made in 5th ch from hook (counts as dc and V-st). *Sk next 2 ch. V-st in next ch. rep from * to last 2 ch. Sk next ch. 1 dc in last ch. Turn. 36 V-sts.

2nd row: Ch 3 (counts as dc). *V-st in next ch-2 sp. Rep from * to last st. 1 dc in top of ch 3. Turn.

Rep last row until work from beg measures 29" [73.5 cm], ending with RS facing for next row.

EDGING

1st rnd: Ch 1. 3 sc in first dc for corner. Work 107 sc along each edge of Blanket and 3 sc in each corner st. Join with sl st to first sc. 440 sc.

2nd rnd: Ch 1. 1 sc in same sp as sl st. [Ch 5. Sk next sc. 1 sc in next corner sc. *Ch 5. Sk next 3 sc. 1 sc in next sc. Rep from * 27 times] 4 times, omitting last sc and join with sl st to first sc.

3rd rnd: Sl st in first ch-5 sp. (Ch 3. 1 dc. Ch 2. 2 dc) in same sp as last sl st. *(2 dc. Ch 2. 2 dc) in next ch-5 sp. rep from * around. Join with sl st to top of ch 3.

4th rnd: Sl st in next dc and ch-2 sp. (Ch 3. 2 dc. Ch 3. 3 dc) in same sp as last sl st. *(3 dc. Ch 3. 3 dc) in next ch-2 sp. rep from * around. Join with sl st to top of ch 3.

5th rnd: Sl st in each of next 2 dc and ch-3 sp. (Ch 3. 3 dc. Ch 3. Sl st in 3rd ch from hook - picot made. 4 dc) in same ch-3 sp. *(4 dc. Picot. 4 dc) in next ch-3 sp. Rep from * around. Join with sl st to top of ch 3. Fasten off. ■

DOUBLE DIAMOND BLANKET

YARN (3)

Bernat® *Softee® Baby™ Solids* 5oz/140g skeins, each approx 362yd/331m (acrylic)

BOY'S VERSION

- A #02002 Pale Blue 2 skeins
- B #02000 White 1 skein
- C #30300 Baby Denim Marl 2 skeins

GIRL'S VERSION

- A #30205 Prettiest Pink 2 skeins
- B #02000 White 1 skein
- C #30301 Baby Pink Marl 2 skeins

HOOK

- Size G-6 (4mm) crochet hook *or size needed to obtain gauge*

MEASUREMENTS

Approx 31" [78.5cm] square.

GAUGE

One Motif = 6" [15cm] square.
Take time to check gauge.

BLANKET

MOTIF A (MAKE 13)

With A, ch 4. Join with sl st to form a ring.

1st rnd: Ch 3 (counts as dc). [3 dc. (Ch 2. 4 dc) 3 times] in ring. Ch 2. Join with sl st to top of ch 3.

2nd rnd: Ch 3 (counts as dc). 1 dc in each of next 3 dc. (2 dc. Ch 2. 2 dc) in next ch-2 sp. *1 dc in each of next 4 dc. (2 dc. Ch 2. 2 dc) in next ch-2 sp. Rep from * twice more. Join with sl st to top of ch 3.

3rd rnd: Ch 3 (counts as dc). *1 dc in each dc to next ch-2 sp. (2 dc. Ch 2. 2 dc) in next ch-2 sp. Rep from * 3 times more. 1 dc in each dc to end of rnd. Join with sl st to top of ch 3.

4th and 5th rnds: As 3rd rnd. (20 dc along each side of Motif after last rnd). Fasten off.

MOTIF B (MAKE 4)

With B, work as given for Motif A.

MOTIF C (MAKE 8)

With C, work as given for Motif A.

FINISHING

Crochet Motifs tog as shown in Diagram.

EDGING

1st rnd: Join B with sl st to any corner sc of Blanket. Work 1 rnd of sc evenly around, having 3 sc in corner ch-2 sps. Join with sl st to first sc.

2nd rnd: Ch 1. 1 sc in every sc around, having 3 sc in corner sc. Join with sl st to first sc. Fasten off. ■

A	A	C	A	A
A	C	B	C	A
C	B	A	B	C
A	C	B	C	A
A	A	C	A	A

QUILT SQUARES BLANKETS

YARN (2)

Bernat® *Baby Coordinates*™ *Solids* 5oz/140g skeins, each approx 388yd/355m; *White* 5oz/140g skeins, each approx 475yd/418m (acrylic/rayon/nylon)

BOY'S VERSION

- MC #48005 White 3 skeins
- A #48128 Soft Blue 2 skeins
- B #48615 Lemon Custard 2 skeins
- C #48228 Iced Mint 2 skeins

GIRL'S VERSION

- MC #48005 White 3 skeins
- A #48320 Soft Mauve 2 skeins
- B #48615 Lemon Custard 2 skeins
- C #48420 Soft Pink 2 skeins

HOOK

- Size G-6 (4mm) crochet hook *or size needed to obtain gauge*

MEASUREMENTS

Approximately 37½ x 46" [95 x 117cm]

GAUGE

15 dc and 7 rows = 4" [10cm] square. *Take time to check gauge.*

MOTIF A (MAKE 7)

With A, ch 2.

1st rnd: (RS) 8 sc in 2nd ch from hook. Join with sl st to first sc.

2nd rnd: Ch 1. 1 sc in same sp as last sl st. *3 sc in next sc. 1 sc in next sc. Rep from * twice more. 3 sc in next sc. Join with sl st to first sc.

3rd rnd: Ch 1. 1 sc in same sp as last sl st. 1 sc in next sc. *3 sc in next sc. 1 sc in each of next 3 sc. Rep from * twice more. 3 sc in next sc. 1 sc in next sc. Join with sl st to first sc.

4th rnd: Ch 1. 1 sc in same sp as last sl st. 1 sc in each of next 2 sc. *3 sc in next sc. 1 sc in each of next 5 sc. Rep from * twice more. 3 sc in next sc. 1 sc in each of next 2 sc. Join with sl st to first sc.

5th rnd: Ch 1. 1 sc in same sp as last sl st. 1 sc in each of next 3 sc. *3 sc in next sc. 1 sc in each of next 7 sc. Rep from * twice more. 3 sc in next sc. 1 sc in each of next 3 sc. Join MC with sl st to first sc.

6th rnd: With MC, ch 3 (counts as dc). Working into back loop only of each st to end of rnd, 1 dc in each of next 4 sc. *5 dc in next sc. 1 dc in each of next 9 sc. Rep from * twice more. 5 dc in next sc. 1 dc in each of next 4 sc. Join with sl st to top of ch 3.

7th rnd: Sl st in next dc. Ch 4 (counts as dc and ch 1). Sk next dc. (1 dc in next dc. Ch 1. Sk next dc) twice. *[(1 dc. Ch 1) twice. 1 dc] all in next dc. (Ch 1. Sk next dc. 1 dc in next dc) 6 times. Ch 1. Sk next dc. Rep from * twice more. [(1 dc. Ch 1) twice. 1 dc] all in next dc. (Ch 1. Sk next dc. 1 dc in next dc) 3 times. Ch 1. Sk next dc. Join with sl st to 3rd ch of ch 4.

8th rnd: Ch 3 (counts as dc). (1 dc in next ch 1 sp. 1 dc in next dc) 3 times. *1 dc in next ch 1 sp. 5 dc in next dc.** (1 dc in next ch 1 sp. 1 dc in next dc) 8 times. Rep from * twice more, then from * to ** once. (1 dc in next ch 1 sp. 1 dc in next dc) 4 times. 1 dc in next ch 1 sp. Join A with sl st to top of ch 3.

9th rnd: With A, ch 3 (counts as dc). Working into back loop only of each st to end of rnd, 1 dc in each of next 9 dc. *5 dc in next dc. 1 dc in each of next 21 dc. Rep from * twice more. 5 dc in next dc. 1 dc in each of next 11 dc. Join with sl st to top of ch 3.

10th rnd: Ch 3. 1 dc in each of next 11 dc. *5 dc in next dc. 1 dc in each of next 25 dc. Rep from * twice more. 5 dc in next dc. 1 dc in each of next 13 dc. Join with sl st to top of ch 3.

11th rnd: Ch 3. 1 dc in each of next 13 dc. *5 dc in next dc. 1 dc in each of next 29 dc. Rep from * twice more. 5 dc in next dc. 1 dc in each of next 15 dc. Join with sl st to top of ch 3. Fasten off.

MOTIF B (MAKE 6)

Work as given for Motif A, substituting B for A.

MOTIF C (MAKE 7)

Work as given for Motif A, substituting C for A.

Following Diagram, sew Motifs into Strips, then Strips into Blanket.

EDGING

1st rnd: Join MC with sl st to top right corner of Blanket. Ch 3. 4 dc in same sp. Working into back loop only of each st to end of rnd, *1 dc in each st across to next corner. 5 dc in next corner. Rep from * twice more. 1 dc in each st across to first corner. Join with sl st to top of ch 3.

2nd and 3rd rnds: Ch 3. 1 dc in each dc across to next corner dc. *5 dc in next corner dc. 1 dc in each dc across to next corner dc. Rep from * 3 times more. Join with sl st to top of ch 3. Fasten off at end of 3rd rnd.

4th rnd: Join A with sl st to first corner dc. Ch 3. 4 dc in same sp. *1 dc in each dc across to next corner dc. 5 dc in next corner dc. Rep from * twice more. 1 dc in each dc across to first corner. Join with sl st to top of ch 3.

5th rnd: Working from left to right instead of from right to left as usual, work 1 reverse sc in each dc around. Join with sl st to first sc. Fasten off. ■

Motif A	Motif B	Motif C	Motif A
Motif C	Motif A	Motif B	Motif C
Motif B	Motif C	Motif A	Motif B
Motif A	Motif B	Motif C	Motif A
Motif C	Motif A	Motif B	Motif C

FAST-AND-COZY BLANKET

YARN (5)
Bernat® *Pipsqueak*™
3½oz/100g skeins, each
approx 120yd/109m
(polyester)
• A #59744 Funny Bunny Print
3 skeins
• B #59005 Whitey White
3 skeins

HOOK
• Size J-10 (6mm) crochet hook
or size needed to obtain gauge

MEASUREMENTS
Approx 40 x 30" [101.5 x 76cm].

GAUGE
8 dc and 4 rows = 4" [10cm].
Take time to check gauge.

INSTRUCTIONS
With A, ch 27.

Foundation rnd: (RS) 2 dc in 3rd ch from hook. (Ch 1. Sk next 3 ch. 3 dc in next ch) 5 times. Ch 1. Sk next 3 ch [(3 dc. Ch 3) twice. 3 dc] in last ch. Working into opposite side of ch (Ch 1. Sk next 3 ch. 3 dc in next ch) 5 times. Ch 1. Sk next 3 ch. (3 dc. Ch 3) twice in last ch. Join B with sl st to top of ch 3.

2nd rnd: With B, sl st in each of first 2 sts. Sl st in next ch-1 sp. Ch 3. 2 dc in same ch-1 sp as sl st. (Ch 1. 3 dc in next ch-1 sp) 5 times. Ch 1. (3 dc. Ch 3. 3 dc) in each of next 2 ch-3 sps. (Ch 1. 3 dc in next ch-1 sp) 6 times. Ch 1. (3 dc. Ch 3. 3 dc) in each of next 2 ch-3 sps. Ch 1. Join A with sl st to top of ch 3.

3rd rnd: With A, sl st in each of first 2 sts. Sl st in next ch-1 sp. Ch 3. 2 dc in same ch-1 sp as sl st. (Ch 1. 3 dc in next ch-1 sp) 6 times. Ch 1. (3 dc. Ch 3. 3 dc) in next ch-3 sp. Ch 1. 3 dc in next ch-1 sp. Ch 1. (3 dc. Ch 3. 3 dc) in next ch-3 sp. (Ch 1. 3 dc in next ch-1 sp) 7 times. Ch 1. (3 dc. Ch 3. 3 dc) in next ch-3 sp. Ch 1. 3 dc in next ch-1 sp. Ch 1. (3 dc. Ch 3. 3 dc) in next ch-3 sp. Ch 1. 3 dc in next ch-1 sp. Ch 1. Join B with sl st to top of ch 3.

Cont in rnds as before, working (Ch 1. 3 dc) in each ch-1 sp and (3 dc. Ch 3. 3 dc) in each corner ch-3 sp, alternating A and B every rnd until longer side of Blanket measures 40" [101.5 cm]. Fasten off. ■

STAR BLANKET

YARN

Bernat® *Baby Coordinates*™ *White* 5oz/140g skeins, each approx 475yd/418m; *Ombres* 4¼oz/120g skeins, each approx 392yd/358m (acrylic/rayon/nylon)

- A #48005 White 1 skein
- B #49415 Candy Baby 2 skeins

HOOK

- Size G-6 (4mm) crochet hook *or size needed to obtain gauge*

MEASUREMENTS

Approximately 38" [96.5cm] diameter

GAUGE

15 dc and 8 rows = 4" [10cm]. *Take time to check gauge.*

BLANKET

Note: Ch 3 at beg of each rnd counts as dc.

With A, ch 4. Join with sl st to form ring.

1st rnd: Ch 6 (counts as 1 dc. Ch 3). (1 dc. Ch 3) 4 times in ring. Join with sl st to 3rd ch of beg ch.

2nd rnd: Sl st in next ch-3 sp. Ch 3. (2 dc. Ch 2. 3 dc) in same sp as last sl st. (3 dc. Ch 2. 3 dc in next ch-3 sp) 4 times. Join with sl st to top of ch 3.

3rd rnd: Sl st in next dc. Ch 3. 1 dc in next dc. *(3 dc. Ch 2. 3 dc) in next ch-2 sp. 1 dc in each of next 2 dc. Sk next 2 dc. 1 dc in each of next 2 dc. Rep from * 4 times more. Join B with sl st to top of ch 3.

4th rnd: With B, sl st in next dc. Ch 3. 1 dc in each of next 3 dc. *(3 dc. Ch 2. 3 dc) in next ch-2 sp. 1 dc in each of next 4 dc. Sk next 2 dc. 1 dc in each of next 4 dc. Rep from * 4 times more. Join with sl st to top of ch 3.

5th rnd: Sl st in next dc. Ch 3. 1 dc in each of next 5 dc. *(3 dc. Ch 2. 3 dc) in next ch-2 sp. 1 dc in each of next 6 dc. Sk next 2 dc. 1 dc in each of next 6 dc. Rep from * 4 times more. Join A with sl st to top of ch 3.

6th rnd: With A, sl st in next dc. Ch 3. 1 dc in each of next 7 dc. *(3 dc. Ch 2. 3 dc) in next ch-2 sp. 1 dc in each of next 8 dc. Sk next 2 dc. 1 dc in each of next 8 dc. Rep from * 4 times more. Join with sl st to top of ch 3.

7th rnd: Sl st in next dc. Ch 3. 1 dc in each of next 9 dc. *(3 dc. Ch 2. 3 dc) in next ch-2 sp. 1 dc in each of next 10 dc. Sk next 2 dc. 1 dc in each of next 10 dc. Rep from * 4 times more. Join B with sl st to top of ch 3.

Cont as established, working 2 more dc before and after each (3 dc. Ch 2. 3 dc) corner in the following sequence: 2 rnds B, 2 rnds A, until Blanket measures approx 38" [96.5 cm] in diameter, ending with 2 rnds of B. Fasten off. ■

HEXAGON MOTIFS BLANKET

YARN (3)

Bernat® *Softee® Baby™ Solids* 5oz/140g skeins, each approx 362yd/331m;
Ombres 4oz/120g skeins, each approx 392yd/358m (acrylic)

- MC #30044 Flannel 3 skeins
- A #31512 Baby Spring *Ombre* 1 skein
- B #30424 Soft Red 1 skein

HOOK

- Size G-6 (4mm) crochet hook *or size needed to obtain gauge*

MEASUREMENTS

Blanket: Approx 33" x 36" [84cm x 91.5cm].

Motif: 6½" [16.5cm] from point to point.

GAUGE

16 sc and 19 rows = 4" [10 cm].
Take time to check gauge.

NOTES

1 When joining colors, work to last 2 loops on hook of first color. Draw new color through last 2 loops and proceed.

2 Ch 3 at beg of rnd counts as dc.

3 Join all rnds with sl st to first st.

BLANKET

MOTIF

(Make 20 with A as Color 1. Make 19 with B as Color 1)

With MC, ch 3. Join with sl st to first ch to form a ring.

1st rnd: Ch 1. 12 sc in ring. Join.

2nd rnd: Ch 3. 1 dc in same sp as last sl st. 2 dc in each sc around. Join. 24 dc.

3rd rnd: Ch 4 (counts as dc and ch 1). (1 dc in next dc. Ch 1) 23 times. Join Color 1. Break MC.

4th rnd: With Color 1, ch 2. (Yoh and draw up a loop) twice in next ch-1 sp. Yoh and draw through all loops on hook – beg cluster made. *Ch 2. (Yoh and draw up a loop) 3 times in next ch-1 sp. Yoh and draw through all loops on hook – cluster made. Rep from * 22 times more. Ch 2. Join. Fasten off.

5th rnd: Join MC to any ch-2 sp. Ch 1. 2 sc in same sp. Ch 1. Sk next cluster st. (2 sc in next ch-2 sp. Ch 1. Sk next cluster st) twice. (1 hdc. 1 dc. Ch 1. 1 dc. 1 hdc) all in next ch-2 sp. Ch 1. Sk next cluster. *(2 sc in next ch-2 sp. Ch 1. Sk next cluster) 3 times. (1 hdc. 1 dc. Ch 1. 1 dc. 1 hdc) all in next ch-2 sp. Ch 1. Sk next cluster. Rep from * 4 times more. Join.

6th rnd: Ch 1. 1 sc in each of next 11 sts. 3 sc in next ch-1 sp. *1 sc in each of next 14 sts. 3 sc in next ch-1 sp. Rep from * 4 times more. 1 sc in each of next 3 sts. Join. Fasten off.

FINISHING

Sew Motifs tog as shown in Diagram. ■

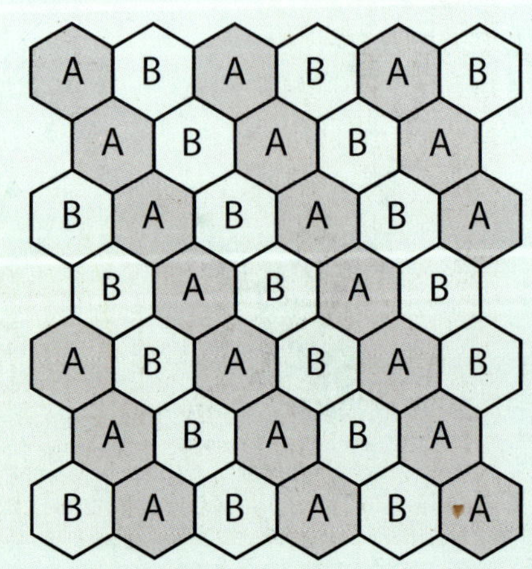

Cont in pat until work from beg measures approx 45" [114.5 cm], ending with row 3 of pat and omitting turning ch at end of last row. Fasten off.

EDGING

Join yarn with sl st at top right corner of Blanket. Ch 3. Work 1 rnd dc around entire Blanket working 3 dc in corners. Join with sl st to top of ch 3. Work 2 more rnds of dc as before. Fasten off. ■

RAINBOW BLANKET

YARN (6)

Bernat® *Tizzy*™
3½oz/100g skeins, each approx 52yd/47m (polyester)

- A #24305 Pixie Purple 2 skeins
- B #24128 Blue Skies 2 skeins
- C #24230 Sweet Green Pea 2 skeins
- D #24611 Dandelion Yellow 2 skeins
- E #24628 Creamsicle 2 skeins
- F #24421 Posey Pink 2 skeins

HOOK

- Size N-15 (10mm) crochet hook *or size needed to obtain gauge*

MEASUREMENTS

Approx 36" [91.5cm] square

GAUGE

5 sc and 6 rows = 4" [10cm].
Take time to check gauge.

NOTE

When joining colors, work to last 2 loops on hook of first color. Draw new color through last 2 loops and proceed.

BLANKET

Work 1 row each of: A, B, C, D, E and F.
These 6 rows form Stripe Pat.
With A, ch 104.

1st row: (RS) 1 sc in 2nd ch from hook. Sk next ch. [(1 sc. Ch 2. 1 sc) in next ch. Sk next 2 ch] 5 times. (1 sc. Ch 2. 1 sc. Ch 3. 1 sc. Ch 2. 1 sc) in next ch. *Sk next 2 ch. [(1 sc. Ch 2. 1 sc) in next ch. Sk next 2 ch] 4 times. 1 sc in next ch. Sk next 3 ch. 1 sc in next ch. Sk next 2 ch. [(1 sc. Ch 2. 1 sc) in next ch. Sk next 2 ch] 4 times. (1 sc. Ch 2. 1 sc. Ch 3. 1 sc. Ch 2. 1 sc) in next ch. Rep from * to last 17 ch. [Sk next 2 ch. (1 sc. Ch 2. 1 sc) in next ch] 5 times. Sk next ch. 1 dc in last ch. Join B. Turn.

2nd row: With B, ch 1. 1 sc in first dc. 1 sc in next ch-2 sp. [(1 sc. Ch 2. 1 sc) in next ch-2 sp] 5 times. (1 sc. Ch 2. 1 sc. Ch 3. 1 sc. Ch 2. 1 sc) in next ch-3 sp. *[(1 sc. Ch 2. 1 sc) in next ch-2 sp] 4 times. 1 sc in next ch-2 sp. Sk next 4 sc. 1 sc in next ch-2 sp. [(1 sc. Ch 2. 1 sc) in next ch-2 sp] 4 times. (1 sc. Ch 2. 1 sc. Ch 3. 1 sc. Ch 2. 1 sc) in next ch -3 sp. Rep from * to last 6 ch-2 sps. [(1 sc. Ch 2. 1 sc) in next ch-2 sp] 5 times. 1 sc in last ch-2 sp. Sk next sc. 1 dc in last sc. Join C. Turn.

Last row forms Ripple Pat.

First 2 rows of Stripe Pat are complete.

Keeping continuity of Stripe pat, cont in Ripple Pat until work from beg measures approx 36" [91.5 cm], ending with 1 row of F. Fasten off. ■

3-COLOR BLANKET

YARN

Bernat® *Baby Sport*™
12.3oz/350g skeins, each approx 1256yd/1148m (acrylic)

- A #21730 Popsicle Blue 1 skein
- B #21230 Baby Green 1 skein
- C #21128 Baby Blue 1 skein

HOOK

- Size G-6 (4mm) crochet hook *or size needed to obtain gauge*

MEASUREMENTS

Approx 43 x 57" [109 x 144.5cm]

GAUGE

16 dc and 9 rows = 4" [10cm].
Take time to check gauge.

STITCH GLOSSARY

Tr2tog (Yoh) twice. Draw up a loop in next ch. (Yoh and draw through 2 loops on hook) twice. Sk next 5 ch. (Yoh) twice. Draw up a loop in next ch. (Yoh and draw through 2 loops on hook) twice. Yoh and draw through all 3 loops on hook.

V-st (1 tr. Ch 5. 1 tr) in next sc.

NOTES

1 Ch 3 at beg of row counts as dc.

2 To change color, work to last 2 loops on hook. Draw loop of next color through 2 loops on hook to complete st and proceed in next color.

STRIP I (MAKE 2)

With A, ch 34.

1st row: (RS) 1 dc in 4th ch from hook. *1 dc in each of next 7 ch. Ch 4. Tr2tog. Ch 4. Rep from * once more. 1 dc in each of last 2 ch. Turn.

****2nd row:** Ch 3. 1 dc in next dc. *Ch 7. 1 dc in each of next 7 dc. Rep from * once more. 1 dc in each of last 2 dc. Turn.

3rd row: Ch 3. 1 dc in next dc. *1 dc in each of next 7 dc. Ch 4. 1 sc in top of Tr2tog 2 rows below, working over ch-7 sp. Ch 4. Rep from * once more. 1 dc in each of last 2 dc. Turn.

4th row: Ch 3. 1 dc in next dc. *V-st. 1 dc in each of next 7 dc. Rep from * once more. 1 dc in each of last 2 dc. Turn.

5th row: Ch 3. 1 dc in next dc. *Ch 4. Tr2tog. Ch 4. 1 dc in next tr. 5 dc in next ch-5 sp. 1 dc in next tr. Rep from * once more. 1 dc in each of last 2 dc. Turn.

6th row: Ch 3. 1 dc in next dc. * 1 dc in each of next 7 dc. Ch 7. Rep from * once more. 1 dc in each of last 2 dc. Turn.

7th row: Ch 3. 1 dc in next dc. *Ch 4. 1 sc in top of Tr2tog 2 rows below, working over ch-7 sp. Ch 4. 1 dc in each of next 7 dc. Rep from * once more. 1 dc in each of last 2 dc. Turn.

8th row: Ch 3. 1 dc in next dc. *1 dc in each of next 7 dc. V-st in next sc. Rep from * once more. 1 dc in each of last 2 dc. Turn.

9th row: Ch 3. 1 dc in next dc. *1 dc in next tr. 5 dc in next ch-5 sp. 1 dc in next tr. Ch 4. Tr2tog over next 7 dc. Ch 4. Rep from * once more. 1 dc in each of last 2 dc. Turn.

Rep 2nd to 4th rows. Break A. With B, rep 5th to 9th rows, then 2nd to 8th rows. Break B. ** With C, rep 9th, then 2nd to 9th rows, then 2nd to 4th rows. Break C.

With A, rep 5th to 9th rows, then 2nd to 8th rows. Break A. With B, rep 9th, then 2nd to 9th rows, then 2nd to 4th rows. Break B. With C, rep 5th to 9th rows, then 2nd to 8th rows. Break C. Join A. With A, rep 9th row. Rep from ** to ** once more. Fasten off at end of last row.

STRIP II (MAKE 2)

With B, ch 34. Work as given for Strip I, substituting B for A, C for B and A for C.

STRIP III (MAKE 2)

With C, ch 34. Work as given for Strip I, substituting C for A, A for B and B for C.

FINISHING

Sew Strips tog in the following sequence: I, II, III, I, II, III.

EDGING

1st rnd: Join A with sl st to any corner of Blanket. Ch 1. Work 1 rnd of sc evenly around Blanket, having

3-COLOR BLANKET

3 sc in corners. Join B with sl st to first sc.

2nd rnd: With B, ch 1. 1 sc in each sc around, having 3 sc in corner sc. Join C with sl st to first sc.

3rd rnd: With C, ch 1. 1 sc in each sc around, having 3 sc in corner sc. Join with sl st to first sc. Fasten off. ■

SWEET STRIPED MINI BLANKET

YARN

Bernat® *Baby Coordinates*™ *Solids* 5oz/140g skeins, each approx 388yd/355m; *White* 5oz/140g skeins, each approx 475yd/418m (acrylic/rayon/nylon)

- MC #01000 White 2 skeins
- A #48412 Sweet Pink 2 skeins

HOOK

- Size G-6 (4mm) crochet hook *or size needed to obtain gauge*

MEASUREMENTS

Approx 20 x 25" [51 x 63.5cm]

GAUGE

19½ sts and 21 rows = 4" [10cm] in pat. *Take time to check gauge.*

STITCH GLOSSARY

2 dc Cluster (Yoh and draw up a loop) 2 times in same stitch or space. Yoh and draw through all loops on hook.

NOTE To change color, work to last 2 loops on hook of last st, then draw new color through rem 2 loops and proceed.

BLANKET

With MC, ch 92.

1st row: (RS) 1 sc in 2nd ch from hook. *Ch 1. Sk next ch. 1 sc in next ch. Rep from * to end of ch. 91 sts. Turn.

2nd row: Ch 1. 1 sc in first sc. *1 sc in next ch-1 sp. Ch 1. Rep from * to last 2 sts. 1 sc in next ch-1 sp. 1 sc in last sc. Join A. Turn.

3rd row: With A, ch 1. 1 sc in first sc. *Ch 1. 1 sc in next ch-1 sp. Rep from * to last sc. 1 sc in last sc.

4th row: With A, as 2nd row.

5th row: With MC, as 3rd row.

Rows 2 to 5 form pat.

Cont in pat until work from beg measures approx 24" [61 cm], ending with 2nd row of pat. Fasten off.

EDGING

With RS of work facing, join A with sl st to top right corner.

1st rnd: Ch 1. 3 sc in same sp as last sl st. 83 sc across top of Blanket. 3 sc in corner. 106 sc down left side of Blanket. 3 sc in corner. 83 sc across bottom of Blanket. 3 sc in corner. 106 sc up right side of Blanket. Join with sl st to first sc.

2nd rnd: Ch 1. (1 sc. Ch 3. 2 dc cluster) all in same sp as last sl st. *Sk next 2 sc. (1 sc. Ch 3. 2 dc cluster) all in next sc. Rep from * around, ending with: sk last 2 sc. Join with sl st to first sc. Fasten off. ■

***Pattern for blanket only.

TEXTURED GRID BLANKET

YARN (3)
Bernat® *Baby Sport*™
12.3oz/350g skeins, each approx 1256yd/1148m (acrylic)
• #21730 Popsicle Blue 1 skein

HOOK
• Size G-6 (4mm) crochet hook
or size needed to obtain gauge

MEASUREMENTS

Approx 28" x 36" [71cm x 91.5cm]

GAUGE

16 sc and 19 rows = 4" [10cm].
Take time to check gauge.

INSTRUCTIONS

Note: Ch 3 at beg of row counts as dc.

Ch 118.

1st row: (WS) 1 dc in 4th ch from hook (counts as 2 dc). *(Ch 2. Sk next 2 ch. 1 dc in each of next 5 ch) twice. Ch 2. Sk next 2 ch. 1 dc in each of next 3 ch. Rep from * 5 times more. Turn.

2nd row: Ch 3. 1 dc in each of next 2 dc. *5 dc in next ch-2 sp. Drop loop from hook. Insert hook from front to back in 1st dc of 5 dc group. Pull dropped loop through. Ch 1 – popcorn made. 1 dc in each of next 5 dc. 2 dc in next ch-2 sp. 1 dc in each of next 5 dc. Popcorn. 1 dc in each of next 3 dc. Rep from * 5 times more. Turn.

3rd row: Ch 3. 1 dc in each of next 2 dc. *Ch 2. Sk next popcorn. 1 dc in each of next 5 dc. Ch 2. Sk next 2 dc. 1 dc in each of next 5 dc. Ch 2. Sk next popcorn. 1 dc in each of next 3 dc. Rep from * 5 times more. Turn.

4th row: Ch 3. 1 dc in each of next 2 dc. *Popcorn. 1 dc in each of next 3 dc. Ch 2. Sk next 2 dc. 1 sc in next ch-2 sp. Ch 2. Sk next 2 dc. 1 dc in each of next 3 dc. Popcorn. 1 dc in each of next 3 dc. Rep from * 5 times more. Turn.

5th row: Ch 3. 1 dc in each of next 2 dc. *Ch 2. Sk next popcorn. 1 dc in each of next 3 dc. 2 dc in next ch-2 sp. Ch 2. Sk next sc. 2 dc in next ch-2 sp. 1 dc in each of next 3 dc. Ch 2. Sk next popcorn. 1 dc in each of next 3 dc. Rep from * 5 times more. Turn.

6th row: Ch 3. 1 dc in each of next 2 dc. *Popcorn. 1 dc in each of next 5 dc. 2 dc in next ch-2 sp. 1 dc in each of next 5 dc. Popcorn. 1 dc in each of next 3 dc. Rep from * 5 times more. Turn.

7th row: Ch 3. 1 dc in each of next 2 dc. *Ch 2. Sk next popcorn. 1 dc in each of next 5 dc. Ch 2. Sk next 2 dc. 1 dc in each of next 5 dc. Ch 2. Sk next popcorn. 1 dc in each of next 3 ch. Rep from * 5 times more. Turn.

Rep 2nd to 7th rows 11 times more. Fasten off.

TASSELS (MAKE 4)

Wind yarn around 4" [10 cm] wide cardboard 50 times. Cut yarn, leaving a long end and thread through a needle. Slip through all loops and tie tightly. Remove from cardboard and wind yarn around loops tightly, approx 1" [2.5 cm] below fold. Fasten securely. Cut through rem loops and trim ends evenly. Sew 1 tassel at each corner of Blanket. ■

CROCODILE STITCH BLANKET

YARN (3)
Bernat® *Softee® Baby™ Solids*
5oz/140g skeins, each approx
362yd/331m (acrylic)
• #02004 Mint 7 skeins

HOOK
• Size I-9 (5.5mm) crochet hook
or size needed to obtain gauge

NOTION
• 7 yds [6.5 m] of contrast color satin ribbon ⅜" [9 mm] wide (optional)

MEASUREMENTS

Approx 35" [89cm] square

GAUGE

6 V-sts and 8 rows = 4" [10cm].
Take time to check gauge.

NOTES

1 The "crocodile stitch" is formed by a 2 row repeat: a row of V-sts followed by a row of scales (or shells). This is a fairly easy pattern to execute and fast to memorize. The novelty of this design is that the scales are crocheted in front of the V-sts with clusters of double crochet (dc) from top to bottom, then from bottom to top, as opposed to working them on top of the row, like in most shell patterns.

2 Ch 3 at beg of rnd counts as dc throughout.

BLANKET

Ch 124.

1st row: (WS) (1 dc. Ch 1. 1 dc) in 7th ch from hook (counts as 1 dc. Ch 1. 1 dc. Ch 1. 1 dc). *Sk next 2 ch. (1 dc. Ch 1. 1 dc) in next ch – V-st made. Rep from * to last 3 ch. Sk next 2 ch. 1 dc in last ch. Turn. 39 V-sts.

2nd row: Ch 3. Work 4 dc down post of first dc of first V-st. Ch 1. Work 5 dc up post of 2nd dc of the same V-st – beg scale st made. *Sk next V-st. Work 5 dc down post of first dc of next V-st. Ch 1. Work 5 dc up post of 2nd dc of the same V-st – scale st made. Rep from * to last dc. Sl st in last dc. Turn. 20 scale sts.

3rd row: Ch 3. V-st in first ch-1 sp of 1st row. *Inserting hook from front to back between next 2 scales and ch-1 sp of 1st row directly behind it, work V-st. Rep from * to last dc. 1 dc in top of last dc of 1st row. Turn. 39 V-sts.

4th row: Sl st in each of first 2 dc and next ch-1 sp. Sk next dc. *Scale st around next V-st. Sk next V-st. Rep from * to last V-st. Sk next dc. Sl st in next ch-1 sp and each of last 2 dc. Turn. 19 scale sts.

5th row: Ch 3. V-st in first ch-1 sp. *V-st in next ch-1 sp. Inserting hook from front to back between next 2 scales and ch-1 sp of 3rd row directly behind it, work V-st. Rep from * to last ch-1 sp. V-st in last ch-1 sp. 1 dc in last dc. Turn. 39 V-sts.

6th row: Ch 1. Scale st around first V-st. *Sk next V-st. Scale st around next V-st. Rep from * to last dc. Sl st in last dc. Turn. 20 scale sts.

Rep 3rd to 6th rows 21 times more, ending on a 6th row. Do not break yarn. There will be 45 rows of scales.

EDGING

1st rnd: (RS) Ch 1. 2 sc in same sp as last sl st. Work 89 sc down left side of Blanket, 3 sc in corner, 119 sc across bottom of Blanket, 3 sc in corner, 89 sc up right side of Blanket, 119 sc across top of Blanket and 1 sc in same sp as first sc. Join with sl st in top of first sc. 428 sc.

2nd rnd: Ch 6 (counts as dc and ch-3). 1 dc in same sp as sl st. *[Ch 1. Sk next sc. 1 dc in next sc. Ch 1. Rep from * to next corner sc, (1 dc. Ch 3. 1 dc) in next corner sc] 3 times. **Ch 1. Sk next sc. 1 dc in next sc. Ch 1. Rep from ** to next corner sc. Join with sl st in 3rd ch of ch 6.

3rd rnd: Sl st in first ch-3 sp. Ch 3. 4 dc in same sp as last sl st. *3 dc in each ch-1 sp to next ch- 3 sp. 5 dc in next ch-3 sp. Rep from * around, ending with 3 dc in each ch-1 sp to next ch-3 sp. Join with sl st in top of ch 3.

4th rnd: Ch 3. 2 dc in each dc around. Join with sl st in top of ch 3.

5th rnd: Ch 3. *2 dc in next dc. 1 dc in next dc. Rep from * around. Join with sl st in top of ch 3. Fasten off.

FINISHING

Optional: Cut 4 pieces of ribbon measuring 60" [152 cm] each. Weave one ribbon piece along each edge of Blanket. Tie bows at each corner. ■

FUZZY SPOTS BLANKET

YARN (5) (6)

Bernat® *Giggles*™ 3½oz/100g skeins, each approx 185yd/169m (acrylic/nylon)

- MC #56005 White 6 skeins

Bernat® *Tizzy*™ 3½oz/100g skeins, each approx 52yd/47m (polyester)

- A #24230 Sweet Green Pea 1 skein
- B #24421 Posey Pink 1 skein
- C #24628 Creamsicle 1 skein
- D #24611 Dandelion Yellow 1 skein

HOOKS

- Sizes I-9 (5.5mm) and N-15 (10mm) crochet hooks

or size needed to obtain gauge

MEASUREMENTS

Approx 36" x 42" [91.5cm x 106.5cm]

GAUGE

12 sc and 13 rows = 4" [10cm] with smaller hook and Bernat® Giggles™. *Take time to check gauge.*

BLANKET

MOTIF

(Make 8 each with A or D as Color 1; Make 7 each with B or C as Color 1)

Note Follow chart on next page or written instructions below.

With Color 1 and larger hook, ch 2.

1st rnd: 6 sc in 2nd ch from hook. Join with sl st to first sc.

2nd rnd: Ch 1. 2 sc in each sc around. Join with sl st to first sc. 12 sc.

3rd rnd: Ch 1. 2 sc in same sc as last sl st. 1 sc in next sc. *(2 sc in next sc) 3 times. 1 sc in next sc. Rep from * once more. (2 sc in next sc) twice. Join with sl st to first sc. 21 sc. Fasten off.

4th rnd: With smaller hook, join MC with sl st in any sc of last rnd. Ch 1. 2 sc in each sc around. Join with sl st to first sc. 42 sc.

5th rnd: Ch 3 (counts as dc). 1 dc in same sp as last sl st. 1 dc in each of next 2 sc. *2 dc in next sc. 1 dc in each of next 2 sc. Rep from * around. Join with sl st to top of ch 3. 56 dc.

6th rnd: Ch 1. 1 sc in same sp as last sl st. 1 sc in next dc. 1 hdc in each of next 2 dc. 1 dc in each of next 2 dc. 1 tr in next dc. *5 tr in next dc. 1 tr in next dc. 1 dc in each of next 2 dc. 1 hdc in each of next 2 dc.** 1 sc in each of next 3 dc. 1 hdc in each of next 2 dc. 1 dc each of next 2 dc. 1 tr in next dc. Rep from * twice more, then from * to ** once. 1 sc in last dc. Join with sl st to first sc.

7th rnd: Ch 2 (does not count as hdc). 1 hdc in same sp as last sl st. 1 hdc in each of next 8 sts. *5 hdc in next st. 1 hdc in each of next 17 sts. Rep from * twice more. 5 hdc in next st. 1 hdc in each of last 8 sts. Join with sl st to first hdc. Fasten off.

FINISHING

With MC, sew Motifs tog as shown in diagram.

EDGING

1st rnd: With RS facing and smaller hook, join MC with sl st in any corner hdc of Blanket. Ch 1. 5 sc in same sp. Work 1 sc in each st around Blanket, working 5 sc in each corner. Join with sl st to first sc.

2nd rnd: Ch 1. Working from left to right, instead of from right to left as usual, work 1 reverse sc in each sc around. Join with sl st to first sc. Fasten off. ■

FUZZY SPOTS BLANKET

Stitch Key

- · slip st
- chain
- \+ single crochet
- half double crochet
- double crochet
- treble crochet

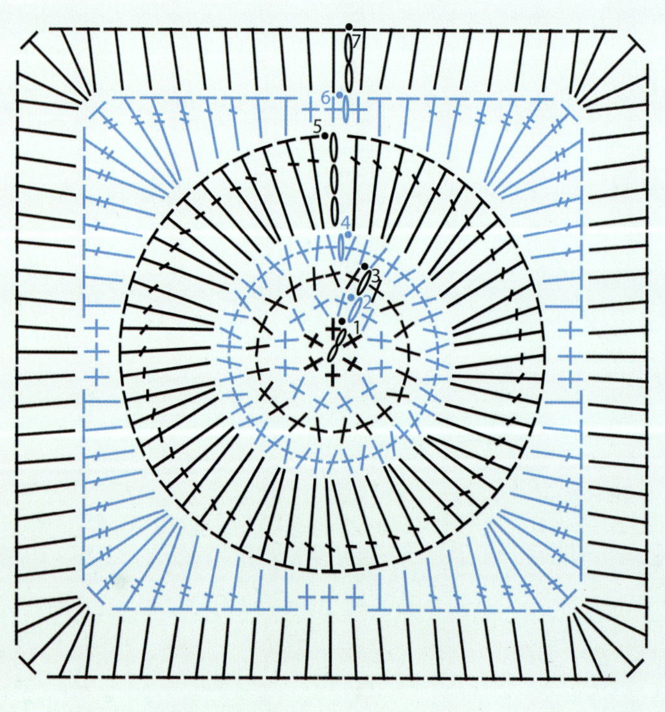

GINGHAM BLANKET

YARN
Bernat® *Baby Coordinates™ Solids* 5oz/140g skeins, each approx 388yd/355m; *White* 5oz/140g skeins, each approx 475yd/418m (acrylic/rayon/nylon)

- A #48131 Blue Bon Bon 2 skeins
- B #48128 Soft Blue 3 skeins
- C #48005 White 1 skein

HOOK
- Size G-6 (4mm) crochet hook

or size needed to obtain gauge

MEASUREMENTS

Approximately 38" [96.5cm] square.

GAUGE

One Motif = 5" [12.5cm] square.
Take time to obtain gauge.

MOTIF

(make 16 with A, 24 with B and 9 with C)

Ch 4. Join with sl st in first ch to form a ring.

1st rnd: Ch 3 (counts as dc). 3 dc in ring. (Ch 3. 4 dc in ring) 3 times. Ch 3. Join with sl st to top of ch 3.

2nd rnd: Ch 5 (counts as dc and ch 2). *Sk next 2 dc. 1 dc in next dc. (2 dc. Ch 3. 2 dc) in next ch-3 sp.** 1 dc in next dc. Ch 2. Rep from * twice more, then from * to ** once. Join with sl st in 3rd ch of ch 5.

3rd rnd: Ch 5. *Sk next ch-2 sp. 1 dc in each of next 3 dc. (2 dc. Ch 3. 2 dc) in next ch-3 sp.** 1 dc in each of next 3 dc. Ch 2. Rep from * twice more, then from * to ** once. 1 dc in each of last 2 dc. Join with sl st in 3rd ch of ch 5.

4th rnd: Ch 5. *Sk next ch-2 sp. 1 dc in each of next 5 dc. (2 dc. Ch 3. 2 dc) in next ch-3 sp.** 1 dc in each of next 5 dc. Ch 2. Rep from * twice more, then from * to ** once. 1 dc in each of last 4 dc. Join with sl st in 3rd ch of ch 5.

5th rnd: Ch 1. 1 sc in same sp as last sl st. *2 sc in next ch-2 sp. 1 sc in each of next 7 dc. 5 sc in next ch-3 sp.** 1 sc in each of next 7 dc. Rep from * twice more, then from * to ** once. 1 sc in each of last 6 dc. Join with sl st to first sc. Fasten off.

FINISHING

Using B, crochet Motifs tog as shown in diagram.

EDGING

1st rnd: (RS) Join C with sl st in any corner sc. Ch 1. 3 sc in same sp. *(Work 21 sc along side of next Motif) 7 times. 3 sc in next corner sc. Rep from * twice more. (Work 21 sc along side of next Motif)

GINGHAM BLANKET

7 times. Join with sl st to first sc. 600 sc.

2nd rnd: Ch 3 (counts as dc). 1 dc in next sc. *Ch 1. Sk next sc. 1 dc in each of next 2 sc. Rep from * to last sc. Ch 1. Sk last sc. Join with sl st to top of ch 3.

3rd rnd: Sl st in next dc. Sl st in next ch-1 sp. Ch 1. 1 sc in same sp. *Ch 4. 1 sc in next ch-1 sp. Rep from * around, ending with ch 4. Join with sl st to first sc.

4th rnd: Sl st in each of next 2 ch. Ch 1. 1 sc in same sp. *5 dc in next ch-4 sp. 1 sc in next ch-4 sp. Rep from * around, ending with 5 dc in last ch-4 sp. Join with sl st to first sc. Fasten off. ■

A	B	A	B	A	B	A
B	C	B	C	B	C	B
A	B	A	B	A	B	A
B	C	B	C	B	C	B
A	B	A	B	A	B	A
B	C	B	C	B	C	B
A	B	A	B	A	B	A

PUZZLE BLOCKS BLANKET

YARN

Bernat® *Baby Coordinates™ Solids* 5oz/140g skeins, each approx 388yd/355m;
White 5oz/140g skeins, each approx 475yd/418m (acrylic/rayon/nylon)

- A #48412 Sweet Pink 2 skeins
- B #48314 Orchid 1 skein
- C #48005 White 1 skein

HOOK

- Size G-6 (4mm) crochet hook *or size needed to obtain gauge*

MEASUREMENTS

Approximately 36" [91.5cm] square

GAUGE

One Motif = 5¾" [14.5cm] square. *Take time to check gauge.*

NOTES

1 Ch 3 at beg of row counts as dc throughout.

2 Follow chart of written instructions below.

MOTIF (MAKE 36)

With B, ch 6.

1st row: 1 dc in 4th ch from hook. 1 dc in each of next 2 ch. Turn.

2nd row: Ch 3. 1 dc in each of next 2 dc. 4 dc in loop made by turning ch of previous row. Turn. 7 dc.

3rd row: Ch 3. 1 dc in each of next 2 dc. (2 dc. Ch 2. 2 dc) in next dc. 1 dc in each of last 3 dc. Join A. Turn.

4th row: With A, ch 4 (counts as dc and ch 1). Sk next dc. 3 dc in next dc. Ch 1. (3 dc. Ch 2. 3 dc) in corner ch-2 sp. Ch 1. Sk next 2 dc. 3 dc in next dc. Ch 1. Sk next dc. 1 dc in last dc. Turn.

5th row: Ch 3. 1 dc in first ch-1sp. Ch 1. 3 dc in next ch-1 sp. Ch 1. (3 dc. Ch 2. 3 dc) in corner ch-2 sp. Ch 1. 3 dc in next ch-1 sp. Ch 1. 1 dc in 4th ch of turning ch. 1 dc in 3rd ch of turning ch. Turn.

6th row: Ch4 (counts as dc and ch 1). (3 dc in next ch-1 sp. Ch 1) twice. (3 dc. Ch 2. 3 dc) in corner ch-2 sp. (Ch 1. 3 dc in next ch-1 sp) twice. Ch 1. Sk next dc. 1 dc in last dc. Join C. Turn.

7th row: With C, ch 3. 1 dc in first ch-1 sp. (Ch 1. 3 dc in next ch-1 sp) twice. Ch 1. (3 dc. Ch 2. 3 dc) in corner ch-2 sp. (Ch 1. 3 dc in next ch-1 sp) twice. Ch 1. 1 dc in 4th ch of turning ch. 1 dc in 3rd ch of turning ch. Join B. Turn.

8th row: With B, ch 4 (counts as dc and ch 1). (3 dc in next ch-1 sp. Ch 1) 3 times. (3 dc. Ch 2. 3 dc) in corner ch-2 sp. (Ch 1. 3 dc in next ch-1 sp) 3 times. Ch 1. Sk next dc. 1 dc in last dc. Join C. Turn.

9th row: With C, ch 3. 1 dc in first ch-1 sp. (Ch 1. 3 dc in next ch-1 sp) 3 times. Ch 1. (3 dc. Ch 2. 3 dc) in corner ch-2 sp. (Ch 1. 3 dc in next ch-1 sp) 3 times. Ch 1. 1 dc in 4th ch of turning ch. 1 dc in 3rd ch of turning ch. Join A. Turn.

10th row: With A, ch 4 (counts as dc and ch 1). (3 dc in next ch-1 sp.

PUZZLE BLOCKS BLANKET

Ch 1) 4 times. (3 dc. Ch 2. 3 dc) in corner ch-2 sp. (Ch 1. 3 dc in next ch-1 sp) 4 times. Ch 1. Sk next dc. 1 dc in last dc. Turn.

11th row: Ch 3. 1 dc in first ch-1 sp. (Ch 1. 3 dc in next ch-1 sp) 4 times. Ch 1. (3 dc. Ch 2. 3 dc) in corner ch-2 sp. (Ch 1. 3 dc in next ch-1 sp) 4 times. Ch 1. 1 dc in 4th ch of turning ch. 1 dc in 3rd ch of turning ch. Fasten off.

FINISHING

Assemble motifs following diagram.

EDGING

1st rnd: (RS) Join C with sl st in any corner ch-2 sp of Blanket. Ch 1. 3 sc in same sp. (Work 22 sc across side of next 6 Motifs. 3 sc in next corner) 3 times. Work 22 sc across side of next 6 Motifs. Join with sl st to first sc. 540 sc.

2nd rnd: Ch 3. 1 dc in same sc as last sl st. *Sk next 2 sc. (1 sc. Ch 3. 1 dc) in next sc. Rep from * around, ending with sk last 2 sc. Join with sl st to first sc. Fasten off. ■

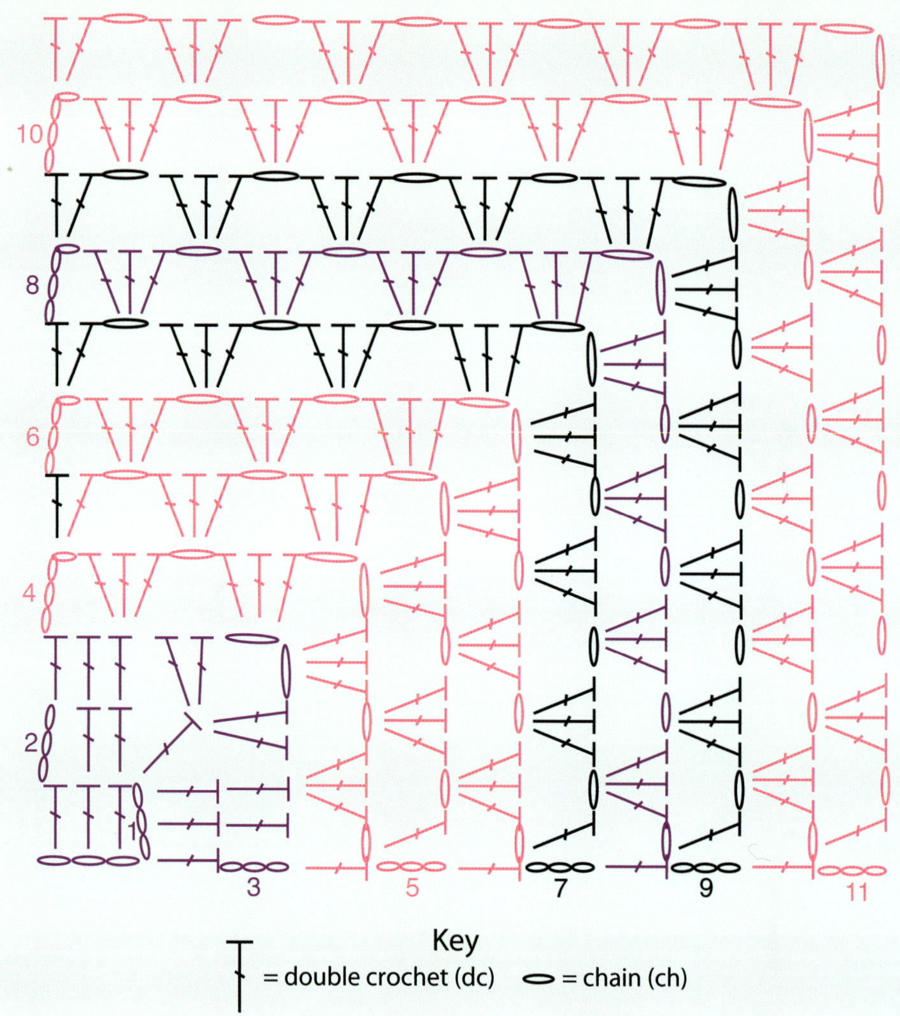

SOFT STRIPES STAR BLANKET

YARN (5)

Bernat® *Pipsqueak*™
3½oz/100g skeins, each approx 120yd/109m (polyester)

- A #59306 Baby Baby Print 2 skeins
- B #59128 Baby Blue 2 skeins
- C #59420 Pretty Pink 2 skeins

HOOK

- Size K-10½ (6.5m) crochet hook *or size needed to obtain gauge*

MEASUREMENTS

Approx 46" [117cm] from point to point

GAUGE

8 dc and 4 rows = 4" [10cm].
Take time to check gauge.

NOTES

1 Carry A loosely up WS of work. Do not break A at end of rnds.

2 Ch 3 at beg of rnds counts as dc throughout.

3 To join new color, work to last 2 loops on hook. Draw new color through last 2 loops then proceed in new color.

BLANKET

With A, ch 6. Join with sl st to form ring.

1st rnd: Ch 3. (1 dc. Ch 2. 1 dc) 5 times in ring. 1 dc in ring. Ch 1. 1 sc in top of ch 3. Join B.

2nd rnd: With B, ch 3. 1 dc around post of last sc. *Ch 1. (2 dc. Ch 2. 2 dc) in next ch-2 sp. Rep from * 4 times more. Ch 1. 2 dc in last ch-1 sp. Ch 1. 1 sc in top of ch 3. Join A.

3rd rnd: With A, ch 3. (1 dc. Ch 2. 2 dc) around post of last sc. *1 hdc in next ch-1 sp. (2 dc. Ch 2. 2 dc) in next ch-2 sp. Rep from * 4 times more. 1 hdc in last ch-1 sp. Join C with sl st to top of ch 3.

4th rnd: With C, sl st in next dc. Ch 3. *(3 dc. Ch 2. 3 dc) in next ch-2 sp. 1 dc in next dc. Sk next dc. 1 hdc in next hdc.** Sk next dc. 1 dc in next dc. Rep from * 4 times more, then from * to ** once. Join A with sl st to top of ch 3.

5th rnd: With A, sl st in next dc. Ch 3. 1 dc in each of next 2 dc. *(3 dc. Ch 2. 3 dc) in next ch-2 sp. 1 dc in each of next 3 dc. Sk next dc. 1 hdc in next hdc.** Sk next dc. 1 dc in each of next 3 dc. Rep from * 4 times more, then from * to ** once. Join B with sl st to top of ch 3.

6th rnd: With B, sl st in next dc. Ch 3. 1 dc in each of next 4 dc. *(3 dc. Ch 2. 3 dc) in next ch-2 sp. 1 dc in each of next 5 dc. Sk next dc. 1 hdc in next hdc.** Sk next dc. 1 dc in each of next 5 dc. Rep from * 4 times more, then from * to ** once. Join A with sl st to top of ch 3.

7th rnd: With A, sl st in next dc. Ch 3. 1 dc in each of next 6 dc. *(3 dc. Ch 2. 3 dc) in next ch-2 sp. 1 dc in each of next 7 dc. Sk next dc. 1 hdc in next hdc.** Sk next dc. 1 dc in each of next 7 dc. Rep from * 4 times more, then from * to ** once. Join C with sl st to top of ch 3.

8th rnd: With C, sl st in next dc. Ch 3. 1 dc in each of next 8 dc. *(3 dc. Ch 2. 3 dc) in next ch-2 sp. 1 dc in each of next 9 dc. Sk next dc. 1 hdc in next hdc.** Sk next dc. 1 dc in each of next 9 dc. Rep from * 4 times more, then from * to ** once. Join A with sl st to top of ch 3.

Keeping continuity of Stripe Pat (A, B, A, C), cont in same manner, having 2 more dc along each side on every rnd until work from center to outer point measures approx 23" [58.5 cm]. Fasten off. ■

MINT LACEY BLANKET

YARN (3)
Bernat® *Softee® Baby™ Solids*
5oz/140g skeins, each approx
362yd/331m (acrylic)
• #02004 Mint 3 skeins

HOOK
• Size G-6 (4mm) crochet hook *or size needed to obtain gauge*

MEASUREMENTS

Approx 38 x 40" [98 x 101.5cm]

GAUGE

2½ reps and 8 rows = 4" [10cm].
Take time to check gauge.

BLANKET

Ch 138.

1st row: (WS) 1 sc in 2nd ch from hook. *Ch 5. Sk next 3 ch. 1 sc in next ch. Rep from * to end of ch. Turn.

2nd row: Ch 5. *1 sc in next ch-5 sp. Ch 2. (Yoh and draw up a loop. Yoh and draw through 2 loops on hook) 3 times in next st. Yoh and draw through all loops on hook—cluster made. Ch 2. 1 sc in next ch-5 sp. Ch 5. Rep from * across, ending with 1 sc in last ch-5 sp. Ch 2. 1 dc in last sc. Turn.

3rd row: Ch 1. 1 sc in first dc. *Ch 5. 1 sc in next cluster. Ch 5. 1 sc in next ch-5 sp. Rep from * across, ending with 1 sc in last turning ch-5 sp. Turn.

4th row: Ch 5. *1 sc in next ch-5 sp. Ch 5. 1 sc in next ch-5 sp. Ch 2. Cluster in next sc. Ch 2. Rep from * across, ending with 1 sc in next ch-5 sp. Ch 2. 1 dc in last sc. Turn.

5th row: Ch 1. 1 sc in first dc. *Ch 5. 1 sc in next ch-5 sp. Ch 5. 1 sc in next cluster. Rep from * across, ending with ch 5. 1 sc in next ch-5 sp. Ch 5. 1 sc in last turning ch-5 sp. Turn.

Rep 2nd to 5th rows for pat until work from beg measures approx 37" [94 cm], ending on a WS row. Cont as follows:

EDGING

1st rnd: Ch 3. 4 dc in first sc. *3 dc in next ch-5 sp. 1 dc in next sc. Rep from * across, working 5 dc in last sc. Work 3 dc in side of each turning ch and 1 dc in side of each sc down side edge. 5 dc in corner. **3 dc in next ch-3 sp on foundation ch. 1 dc in rem loop below sc on foundation ch. Rep from ** across, working 5 dc in last sc. Work 3 dc in side of each turning ch and 1 dc in side of each sc up side edge. Join with sl st to top of ch 3.

2nd rnd: Ch 4. 1 dc in next dc. (Ch 1. 1 dc in next dc) twice. *Ch 1. Sk next dc. 1 dc in next dc. Rep from * to next corner 5 dc. (Ch 1. 1 dc in next dc) 4 times. ** Rep from * to ** twice more. ***Ch 1. Sk next dc. 1 dc in next dc. Rep from *** to end of rnd, ending with ch 1. Sk last dc. Join with sl st to 3rd ch of ch 4.

3rd rnd: Ch 1. 1 sc in same sp as last sl st. *Ch 2. Sk next ch-1 sp. Cluster in next dc. Ch 2. Sk next ch-1 sp. 1 sc in next dc. Rep from * around, ending with ch 2. Sk last ch-1 sp. Sl st in first sc. Fasten off. ■

DAISY BLANKET

YARN (3)

Bernat® *Softee® Baby™ Solids*
5oz/140g skeins, each approx
362yd/331m (acrylic)

- A #30233 Fresh Green 1 skein
- B #30221 Soft Fern 1 skein
- C #02003 Lemon 1 skein
- D #02000 White 1 skein

HOOKS

- Sizes E-4 (3.5mm) and G-6 (4mm) crochet hook

or size needed to obtain gauge

NOTIONS

- Stuffing
- Black embroidery floss

MEASUREMENTS

Approx 36" [91.5cm] square

GAUGE

17 dc and 10 rows = 4" [10cm] with larger hook.
Take time to check gauge.

STRIPE PAT

With A, work 2 rows.
With B, work 2 rows.
With C, work 2 rows.
With D, work 2 rows.

NOTES

1 To change colors, work to last 2 loops on hook. Drop previous color from hook, draw new color through and proceed.

2 Ch 3 at beg of dc rows counts as dc throughout.

BLANKET

With larger hook and A, ch 5.

1st row: (RS) 2 dc in 4th ch from hook (counts as 3 dc). 2 dc in next ch. 5 dc. Turn.

2nd row: Ch 3. 2 dc in first st (2 inc made). 1 dc in each of next 3 sts. 3 dc in last st (2 inc made). 9 dc. Join B. Turn.

3rd row: With B, ch 3. 2 dc in first st (2 inc made). 1 dc in each dc to last dc. 3 dc in last st (2 inc made). Turn. 13 dc.

3 rows of Stripe Pat are complete. Keeping continuity of Stripe Pat, rep last row until side edges measure approx 36" [91.5 cm].

Decrease as follows:

Next row: Ch 3. (Yoh and draw up a loop in next dc. Yoh and draw through 2 loops on hook) twice. Yoh and draw through all loops on hook - dc2tog made. 1 dc in each st to last 3 sts. (Yoh and draw up a loop in next dc. Yoh and draw through 2 loops on hook) 3 times. Yoh and draw through all loops on hook - dc3tog made. Turn.

Keeping continuity of Stripe Pat, rep last row to 5 sts.

Next row: Ch 3. Dc2tog. 1 dc in next dc. Dc2tog. Turn.

Next row: Ch 3. Dc3tog. Fasten off.

EDGING

1st rnd: (RS) With larger hook, join D with sl st in any corner. Ch 1. Work 1 rnd sc evenly around Blanket, working 3 sc in each corner. Join with sl st to first sc.

2nd rnd: Ch 1. Working from left to right, instead of from right to left as usual, work 1 reverse sc in each sc around. Join with sl st to first reverse sc. Fasten off.

FLOWER

CENTER (MAKE 2)

With smaller hook and D, ch 2.

1st rnd: (RS) 8 sc in 2nd ch from hook. Join with sl st to first sc.

2nd rnd: Ch 1. *2 sc in next sc. Rep from * around. Join with sl st to first sc. 16 sc.

3rd rnd: Ch 1. *1 sc in next sc. 2 sc in next sc. Rep from * around. Join with sl st to first sc. 24 sc.

4th rnd: Ch 1. *2 sc in next sc. 1 sc in each of next 2 sc. Rep from * around. Join with sl st to first sc. 32 sc.

5th rnd: Ch 1. *1 sc in each of next 3 sc. 2 sc in next sc. Rep from * around. Join with sl st to first sc. 40 sc.

6th rnd: Ch 1. *1 sc in each of next 2 sc. 2 sc in next sc. 1 sc in each of next 2 sc. Rep from * around. Join with sl st to first sc. 48 sc.

7th rnd: Ch 1. *1 sc in each of next 5 sc. 2 sc in next sc. Rep from * around. Join with sl st to first sc. 56 sc.

8th rnd: Ch 1. *1 sc in each of next 3 sc. 2 sc in next sc. 1 sc in each of next 3 sc. Rep from * around. Join with sl st to first sc. 64 sc.

9th rnd: Ch 1. *1 sc in each of next 7 sc. 2 sc in next sc. Rep from * around.

DAISY BLANKET

Join with sl st to first sc. 72 sc.

10th rnd: Ch 1. *1 sc in each of next 4 sc. 2 sc in next sc. 1 sc in each of next 4 sc. Rep from * around. Join with sl st to first sc. 80 sc.

11th rnd: Ch 1. *1 sc in each of next 9 sc. 2 sc in next sc. Rep from * around. Join with sl st to first sc. 88 sc.

12th rnd: Ch 1. *1 sc in each of next 5 sc. 2 sc in next sc. 1 sc in each of next 5 sc. Rep from * around. Join with sl st to first sc. 96 sc. Fasten off.

Place WS of Center pieces tog. Join C with sl st at edge and work 1 rnd of sc around, leaving an opening for stuffing. Stuff Center lightly. Crochet opening closed. Fasten off.

PETALS (MAKE 6)

With smaller hook and C, ch 4.

1st rnd: 11 dc in 4th ch from hook. Join with sl st to top of ch 3. 12 dc.

2nd rnd: Ch 3 (counts as dc). 1 dc in same sp as last sl st. 2 dc in each dc around. Join with sl st to top of ch 3. 24 dc.

3rd rnd: Ch 3 (counts as dc). 1 dc in same sp as last sl st. *1 dc in next dc. 2 dc in next dc. Rep from * around to last dc. 1 dc in last dc. Join with sl st to top of ch 3. 36 dc.

4th rnd: With B, ch 3 (counts as dc). 1 dc in same sp as last sl st. *1 dc in next dc. 2 dc in next dc. Rep from * around to last dc. 1 dc in last dc. Join with sl st to top of ch 3. 54 dc.

Do not break yarn.

Fold Petal in half with WS tog and beg of rnd at edge of fold.

Next row: Ch 1. Working through both thicknesses, work 1 row of sc across open edge to join. Do not turn.

Next row: Ch 1. Working from left to right, instead of from right to left as usual, work 1 reverse sc in each sc around. Join with sl st to first sc. Fasten off.

LEAVES (MAKE 2)

With smaller hook and A, ch 18.

1st row: (RS) 1 dc in 4th ch from hook (counts as 2 dc). 1 dc in each ch to last ch. 5 dc in last ch. Working in rem loops of foundation ch across opposite side of ch, work 1 sc in each of next 15 sts. Turn.

2nd row: Sl st in each of first 4 dc. Ch 3 (counts as dc). 1 dc in each of next 13 dc. 5 dc in next dc. 1 dc in each of next 14 dc. Turn.

3rd row: Sl st in each of first 4 dc. Ch 3 (counts as dc). 1 dc in each of next 12 dc. 5 dc in next dc. 1 dc in each of next 13 dc. Turn.

4th row: Sl st in each of first 4 dc. Ch 3 (counts as dc). 1 dc in each of next 11 dc. 5 dc in next dc. 1 dc in each of next 12 dc. Fasten off.

FINISHING

Sew Petals evenly around edge of Center, gathering in fullness. Sew Leaves to Center behind Petals as seen in picture. With embroidery floss, embroider eyes using satin stitch and mouth using chain stitch. Sew Flower to corner of Blanket. ■

PRETTY FLOWERS BLANKET

YARN (3)

Bernat® *Softee® Baby™ Solids* 5oz/140g skeins, each approx 362yd/331m;
Ombres 4oz/120g skeins, each approx 392yd/358m (acrylic)

- MC #31415 Candy Baby Ombre 3 skeins
- A #30424 Soft Red 1 skein

HOOKS

- Sizes G-6 (4mm) and H-8 (5mm) crochet hook *or size needed to obtain gauge*

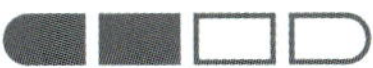

MEASUREMENTS

Approx 32" [81.5cm] square

GAUGES

18 sc and 19 rows = 4" [10cm] with smaller hook.
17 sc and 18 rows = 4" [10cm] with larger hook.
Take time to check gauges.

NOTE

Instructions are for blanket only.

BLANKET

With larger hook and MC, ch 99.
1st row: (RS) 1 sc in 3rd ch from hook (counts as dc and sc). *Ch 3. Sk next ch. 1 dc in next ch. 1 sc in next ch. Rep from * to end of ch. 32 ch-3 sps. Turn.
2nd row: Ch 3 (counts as dc). *1 sc in next dc. Ch 3. 1 dc in next sc. Rep from * to last st. 1 sc in top of turning ch. Turn.
Rep last row for pat until work from beg measures 32" [81.5cm], ending with a WS row. Fasten off.

EDGINGS (MAKE 4)

With larger hook and A, ch 106.
1st row: (RS) 1 sc in 2nd ch from hook. *Ch 5. Sk next 3 ch. Sl st in next ch. (Ch 4. 1 tr. Ch 4. Sl st) twice in same sp as last sl st. Ch 5. Sk next 3 ch. Sl st in next ch. Rep from * to end of ch.** Do not turn. Working in rem loops of opposite side of foundation ch, rep from * to ** once. Fasten off.
Sew edgings along 4 sides 1" [2.5cm] in from edges of Blanket. ■

MESH BLANKET

YARN (3)

Bernat® *Softee® Baby™ Solids* 5oz/140g skeins, each approx 362yd/331m (acrylic)
• #02002 White 3 skeins

HOOKS

• Sizes F-5 (3.75mm) and G-6 (4mm) crochet hooks
or size needed to obtain gauge

MEASUREMENTS

Approx 32½ x 40" [82.5 x 101.5cm]

GAUGE

Blanket: 2½ reps and 8 rows = 4" [10cm] with larger hook in pat.
Take time to check gauge.

BLANKET

With larger hook, ch 138.

1st row: (WS) 1 sc in 2nd ch from hook. *Ch 5. Sk next 3 ch. 1 sc in next ch. Rep from * across. Turn.

2nd row: Ch 5. *1 sc in next ch-5 sp. Ch 2. (Yoh and draw up a loop. Yoh and draw through 2 loops on hook) 3 times in next sc. Yoh and draw through all loops on hook – cluster made. Ch 2. 1 sc in next ch-5 sp. Ch 5. Rep from * across, ending with 1 sc in last ch-5 sp. Ch 2. 1 dc in last sc. Turn.

3rd row: Ch 1. 1 sc in first dc. *Ch 5. 1 sc in next cluster. Ch 5. 1 sc in next ch-5 sp. Rep from * across, ending with 1 sc in last turning ch-5 sp. Turn.

4th row: Ch 5. *1 sc in next ch-5 sp. Ch 5. 1 sc in next ch-5 sp. Ch 2. Cluster in next sc. Ch 2. Rep from * across ending with 1 sc in next ch-5 sp. Ch 2. 1 dc in last sc. Turn.

5th row: Ch 1. 1 sc in first dc. *Ch 5. 1 sc in next ch-5 sp. Ch 5. 1 sc in next cluster. Rep from * across, ending with Ch 5. 1 sc in next ch-5 sp. Ch 5. 1 sc in last turning ch-5 sp. Turn.

Rep 2nd to 5th rows for pat until work from beg measures approx 37" [94cm] ending on a WS row.

EDGING

1st rnd: Ch 3. 4 dc in first sc. *3 dc in next ch-5 sp. 1 dc in next sc. Rep from * across working 5 dc in last sc. Work 3 dc in sides of each turning ch and 1 dc in side of each sc along side. 5 dc in corner. **3 dc in next ch-3 sp on foundation ch. 1 dc in rem loop below sc on foundation ch. Rep from ** across working 5 dc in last sc. Work 3 dc in sides of each turning ch and 1 dc in side of each sc along side. Join with sl st to top of ch 3.

2nd rnd: Ch 4. 1 dc in next dc. (Ch 1. 1 dc in next dc) twice. *Ch 1. Sk next dc. 1 dc in next dc. Rep from * to next corner 5 dc. (Ch 1. 1 dc in next dc) 4 times.** Rep from * to ** twice more. ***Ch 1. Sk next dc. 1 dc in next dc. Rep from *** to end of rnd, ending with ch 1. Sk last dc. Join with sl st to 3rd ch of ch 4.

3rd rnd: Ch 1. 1 sc in same sp as last sl st. *Ch 2. Sk next ch-1 sp. Cluster in next dc. Ch 2. Sk next ch-1 sp. 1 sc in next dc. Rep from * around, ending with ch 2. Sk last ch-1 sp. Sl st in first sc. Fasten off. ■

Shhh...
Baby is
Sleeping

LACY STRIPED BLANKET

YARN

Bernat® *Softee® Baby™ Solids*
5oz/140g skeins, each approx
362yd/331m (acrylic)
• A #02001 Pink 3 skeins
• B #30044 Flannel 2 skeins

HOOK

• Size G-6 (4mm) crochet hook
or size needed to obtain gauge

MEASUREMENT

Approx 38" [96.5cm] square.

GAUGE

18 sc and 19 rows = 4" [10cm].
Take time to check gauge.

BLANKET

PANEL (MAKE 11)

With A, ch 18.

1st row: (RS) 1 sc in 11th ch from hook (turning ch counts as ch 4, 1 dc and ch 4). Ch 3. Sk next ch. 1 sc in next ch. Ch 3. Sk next 4 ch. 1 dc in last ch. Turn.

2nd row: Ch 5 (counts as dc and ch 2). 1 sc in ch-4 sp. Ch 1. 7 dc in ch-3 sp. Ch 1. 1 sc in next ch-4 sp. Ch 2. 1 dc in 3rd ch of ch 5. Turn.

3rd row: Ch 4 (counts as dc and ch 1). (Yoh and draw up a loop. Yoh and draw through 2 loops on hook) 4 times in next dc. Yoh and draw through all loops on hook – cluster made. (Ch 3. Sk next dc. Cluster in next dc) 3 times. Ch 1. 1 dc in 3rd ch of ch 5. Turn.

4th row: Ch 5 (counts as dc and ch 2). 1 sc in first ch-3 sp. (Ch 3. 1 sc in next ch-3 sp) twice. Ch 2. 1 dc in 3rd ch of ch 4. Turn.

5th row: Ch 7 (counts as dc and ch 4). 1 sc in next ch-3 sp. Ch 3. 1 sc in next ch-3 sp. Ch 4. 1 dc in 3rd ch of ch 5. Turn.

Rep 2nd to 5th rows until work from beg measures approx 36" [91.5 cm] ending on a 5th row. Fasten off.

EDGING

With RS facing, join B with sl st in center ch-1 sp of bottom foundation ch. Ch 3 (counts as dc). 2 dc in same sp. 4 dc in next ch-4 sp. 3 dc in corner. Work 2 dc in each ch-3 sp or around side of each dc up side of Panel to next corner. 3 dc in corner. 4 dc in ch-4 sp. 3 dc in center ch-3 sp. 4 dc in ch-4 sp. 3 dc in corner. Work 2 dc in each ch-3 sp or around side of each dc down side of Panel to next corner. 3 dc in corner. 4 dc in last ch-4 sp. Join with sl st to top of ch 3. Fasten off.

JOIN PANELS

Place WS of Panels tog. With RS facing, join B with sl st in corner dc at bottom edge (working through both thicknesses). Ch 1. 1 sc in same sp. Work 1 sc in each dc up side (working through both thicknesses) to corner dc. Fasten off. ■

STAR BLANKET

YARN 5

Bernat® *Pipsqueak*™
3½oz/100g skeins, each approx 120yd/109m (polyester)

- A #59128 Baby Blue 3 skeins
- B #59005 Whitey White 3 skeins

HOOK

- Size K-10½ (6.5m) crochet hook *or size needed to obtain gauge*

MEASUREMENTS

Approx 40" [101.5cm] from point to point

GAUGE

10 dc and 6 rows = 4" [10cm].
Take time to check gauge.

BLANKET

Note: Ch 3 at beg of rnd counts as dc throughout.

Beg at center, with A, ch 5. Join with sl st to form ring.

1st rnd: Ch 2 (does not count as st). 12 hdc in ring. Join with sl st to first hdc. 12 dc.

2nd rnd: Ch 1. 1 sc in same sp as last sl st. *3 dc in next hdc. 1 sc in next hdc. Rep from * around to last hdc. 3 hdc in last hdc. Join B with sl st to first sc.

3rd rnd: With B, sl st in next dc. Ch 3. (2 dc. Ch 2. 2 dc) in next dc. 1 dc in next dc. *Sk next sc. 1 dc in next dc. (2 dc. Ch 2. 2 dc) in next dc. 1 dc in next dc. Rep from * 4 times more. Join A with sl st to top of ch 3.

4th rnd: With A, sl st in next dc. Ch 3. 1 dc in next dc. *(2 dc. Ch 2. 2 dc) in next ch-2 sp. 1 dc in each of next 2 dc.** Draw up a loop in each of next 2 dc. Yoh and draw through all loops on hook – sc2tog made. 1 dc in each of next 2 dc. Rep from * 4 times more, then from * to ** once. Sc2tog over last 2 sts. Join with sl st to top of ch 3.

5th rnd: Ch 3. 1 dc in each of next 3 dc. *(2 dc. Ch 2. 2 dc) in next ch-2 sp. 1 dc in each of next 4 dc.** Sk next st. 1 dc in each of next 4 dc. Rep from * 4 times more, then from * to ** once. Sk last st. Join B with sl st to top of ch 3.

6th rnd: With B, sl st in next dc. Ch 3. 1 dc in each of next 3 dc. *(2 dc. Ch 2. 2 dc) in next ch-2 sp. 1 dc in each of next 5 dc.** Sc2tog over next 2 dc. 1 dc in each of next 5 dc. Rep from * 4 times more, then from * to ** once. Sc2tog over last 2 dc. Join A with sl st to top of ch 3.

7th rnd: With A, ch 3. 1 dc in each of next 6 dc. *(2 dc. Ch 2. 2 dc) in next ch-2 sp. 1 dc in each of next 7 dc.** Sk next st. 1 dc in each of next 7 dc. Rep from * 4 times more, then from * to ** once. Sk last st. Join with sl st to top of ch 3.

8th rnd: Sl st in next dc. Ch 3. 1 dc in each of next 7 dc. *(2 dc. Ch 2. 2 dc) in next ch-2 sp. 1 dc in each of next 8 dc.** Sc2tog over next 2 dc. 1 dc in each of next 8 dc. Rep from * 4 times more, then from * to ** once. Sc2tog over last 2 dc. Join B with sl st to top of ch 3.

9th rnd: With B, ch 3. 1 dc in each of next 9 dc. *(2 dc. Ch 2. 2 dc) in next ch-2 sp. 1 dc in each of next 10 dc.** Sk next st. 1 dc in each of next 10 dc. Rep from * 4 times more, then from * to ** once. Sk last st. Join A with sl st to top of ch 3.

10th rnd: With A, sl st in next dc. Ch 3. 1 dc in each of next 10 dc. *(2 dc. Ch 2. 2 dc) in next ch-2 sp. 1 dc in each of next 11 dc.** Sc2tog over next 2 dc. 1 dc in each of next 11 dc. Rep from * 4 times more, then from * to ** once. Sc2tog over last 2 dc. Join with sl st to top of ch 3.

11th rnd: Ch 3. 1 dc in each of next 12 dc. *(2 dc. Ch 2. 2 dc) in next ch-2 sp. 1 dc in each of next 13 dc.** Sk next st. 1 dc in each of next 13 dc. Rep from * 4 times more, then from * to ** once. Sk last st. Join B with sl st to top of ch 3.

Cont as established, (working 1 rnd B; 2 rnds A throughout) until work from center to outer point measures approx 20" [51 cm], ending with 2 rnds of A. Fasten off. ■

BEAR PUPPET BLANKIE

YARN (3)

Bernat® *Softee® Baby™ Solids* 5oz/140g skeins, each approx 362yd/331m (acrylic)

- A #02002 Pale Blue 4 skeins
- B #02000 White 3 skeins

HOOKS

- Sizes G-6 (4mm) and H-8 (5mm) crochet hook

or size needed to obtain gauge

NOTIONS

- Stuffing
- 12" [30.5cm] square of white felt

MEASUREMENTS

Approx 34" [86.5cm] square

GAUGE

16 dc and 8 rows = 4" [10cm] with larger hook. *Take time to check gauge*

BLANKET

Beg at center of Blanket, with A and larger hook, ch 24. Join with sl st to first ch.

Foundation rnd: (RS) Ch 3. (Yoh and draw up a loop in same sp as sl st. Yoh and draw through 2 loops on hook) twice. Yoh and draw through all 3 loops on hook – Beg Cluster made. Ch 3. (Yoh and draw up a loop. Yoh and draw through 2 loops on hook) 3 times in same sp as sl st. Yoh and draw through all 4 loops on hook – Cluster made. *Ch 1. Sk next 2 ch. 1 dc in next ch. Ch 1. Sk next 2 ch. (Cluster. Ch 3. Cluster) in next ch. Rep from * twice more. Ch 1. Sk next 2 ch. 1 dc in next ch. Ch 1. Sk last 2 ch. Join B with sl st to top of Beg Cluster.

2nd rnd: With B, sl st in next ch-3 sp. (Beg Cluster. Ch 3. Cluster) in same sp as sl st. *Ch 1. 1 dc in next cluster. Ch 1. Cluster in next dc. Ch 1. 1 dc in next cluster. Ch 1.** (Cluster. Ch 3. Cluster) in next ch-3 sp. Rep from * twice more, then from * to ** once. Join A with sl st to top of Beg Cluster.

3rd rnd: With A, sl st in next ch-3 sp. (Beg Cluster. Ch 3. Cluster) in same sp as sl st. *Ch 1. 1 dc in next Cluster. Ch 1. Cluster in next dc.** Rep from * to ** to next corner. Ch 1. 1 dc in next Cluster. Ch 1. (Cluster. Ch 3. Cluster) in next ch-3 sp. Rep from * twice more, then from * to ** once. Ch 1. 1 dc in next Cluster. Join B with sl st to top of Beg Cluster.

Rep last rnd, alternating colors A and B until Blanket measures approx 30" [76cm] wide, ending with A. Fasten off.

BEAR HEAD

With smaller hook and A, ch 4. Join with sl st to first ch to form a ring.

****1st rnd:** Ch 1. 6 sc in ring. Join with sl st to first sc.

2nd rnd: Ch 1. 2 sc in each sc around. Join with sl st to first sc. 12 sc.

3rd rnd: Ch 1. *2 sc in next sc. 1 sc in next sc. Rep from * around. Join with sl st to first sc. 18 sc.

4th rnd: Ch 1. *2 sc in next sc. 1 sc in each of next 2 sc. Rep from * around. Join with sl st to first sc. 24 sc.

5th rnd: Ch 1. *2 sc in next sc. 1 sc in each of next 3 sc. Rep from * around. Join with sl st to first sc. 30 sc.

6th rnd: Ch 1. *2 sc in next sc. 1 sc in each of next 4 sc. Rep from * around. Join with sl st to first sc. 36 sc.

7th rnd: Ch 1. *2 sc in next sc. 1 sc in each of next 5 sc. Rep from * around. Join with sl st to first sc. 42 sc.

8th rnd: Ch 1. *2 sc in next sc. 1 sc in each of next 6 sc. Rep from * around. Join with sl st to first sc. 48 sc.**

9th rnd: Ch 1. *2 sc in next sc. 1 sc in each of next 7 sc. Rep from * around. Join with sl st to first sc. 54 sc.

10th rnd: Ch 1. *2 sc in next sc. 1 sc in each of next 8 sc. Rep from * around. Join with sl st to first sc. 60 sc.

11th rnd: Ch 1. 1 sc in each sc around. Join with sl st to first sc. Place marker at end of rnd.

Rep last rnd until work from marked rnd measures 3" [7.5cm].

Next rnd: Ch 1. *Draw up a loop in each of the next 2 sts. Yoh and draw through all 3 loops on hook – sc2tog made. 1 sc in each of next 8 sc. Rep from * around. Join with sl st to first sc. 54 sts.

Next rnd: Ch 1. *Sc2tog over next 2 sts. 1 sc in each of next 7 sc. Rep from * around. Join with sl st to first sc. 48 sts.

Next rnd: Ch 1. *Sc2tog over next 2 sts. 1 sc in each of next 6 sc. Rep

BEAR PUPPET BLANKIE

from * around. Join with sl st to first sc. 42 sts.

Cont in same manner, dec 6 sts on every rnd 3 times more. 24 sts. Fasten off.

ARMS (MAKE 2)

With smaller hook and A, ch 4. Join with sl st to first ch to form a ring. Work from ** to ** as given for Head.

9th to 11th rnds: Ch 1. 1 sc in each sc around. Join with sl st to first sc.

12th rnd: Ch 1. *Sc2tog over next 2 sts. 1 sc in each of next 6 sc. Rep from * around. Join with sl st to first sc. 42 sts.

13th rnd: Ch 1. *Sc2tog over next 2 sts. 1 sc in each of next 5 sc. Rep from * around. Join with sl st to first sc. 36 sts.

14th rnd: Ch 1. *Sc2tog over next 2 sts. 1 sc in each of next 4 sc. Rep from * around. Join with sl st to first sc. 30 sts.

15th rnd: Ch 1. *Sc2tog over next 2 sts. 1 sc in each of next 3 sc. Rep from * around. Join with sl st to first sc. 24 sts.

16th rnd: Ch 1. *Sc2tog over next 2 sts. 1 sc in each of next 2 sc. Rep from * around. Join with sl st to first sc. 18 sts. Fasten off.

MUZZLE

Work from ** to ** as given for Head.

9th rnd: Ch 1. 1 sc in each sc around. Join with sl st to first sc. Fasten off.

EARS (MAKE 2)

With smaller hook and A, ch 8.

1st row: (RS) 1 sc in 2nd ch from hook and each ch to end of ch. Turn. 7 sc.

2nd and 3rd rows: Ch 1. 1 sc in each sc to end of row. Turn.

4th row: Ch 1. Sc2tog over first 2 sc. 1 sc in each of next 3 sc. Sc2tog over last 2 sts. Turn.

5th row: Ch 1. Sc2tog over first 2 sc. 1 sc in next sc. Sc2tog over last 2 sts. Fasten off.

EDGING

With RS of work facing, join A with sl st to bottom right corner at foundation ch.

1st row: Ch 1. 1 sc in same sp as sl st. Work 13 sc across shaped edge of Ear to opposite left bottom corner. Do not turn.

2nd row: Ch 1. Working from left to right, instead of from right to left as usual, work 1 reverse sc in each sc to end of row. Fasten off.

FINISHING

Stuff Arms and Head. Cut felt, using diagram below (2 pieces for Head, 4 pieces for Arms). Sew sides of felt (see diagram). Insert felt into Arms and Head. Sew edges of felt and Arm closed. Sew edges of felt and Head closed. Sew Head into center of Blanket, matching foundation chain of Blanket with opening of Head. Try to insert 2 fingers into Head opening (it should fit comfortably). Sew Arms at each side of Head, matching opening of Arm with hole between clusters. Try to insert one finger into Arm opening (it should fit comfortably).

Sew on Ears. With B, embroider eyes and nose. ■

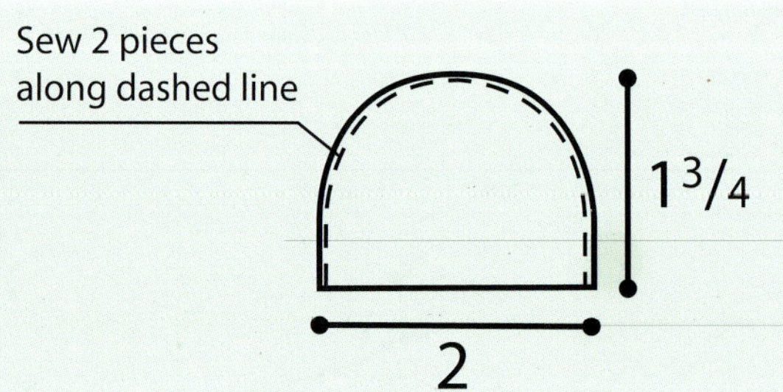